TATTOO
COLORING BOOK
FOR ADULTS

40 MODERN AND NEO-TRADITIONAL TATTOO DESIGNS INCLUDING SUGAR SKULLS, MANDALAS AND MORE

ADULT COLORING WORLD

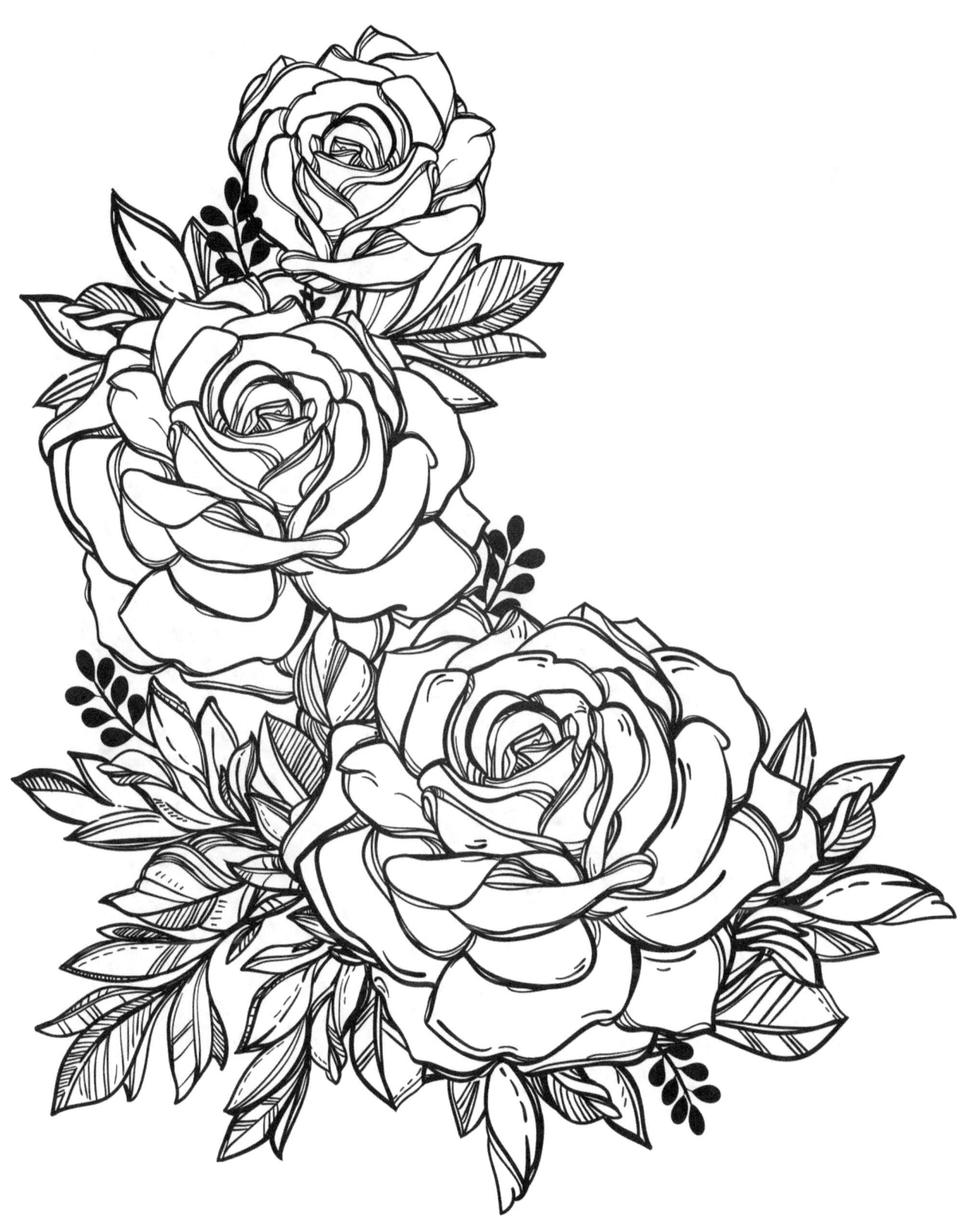

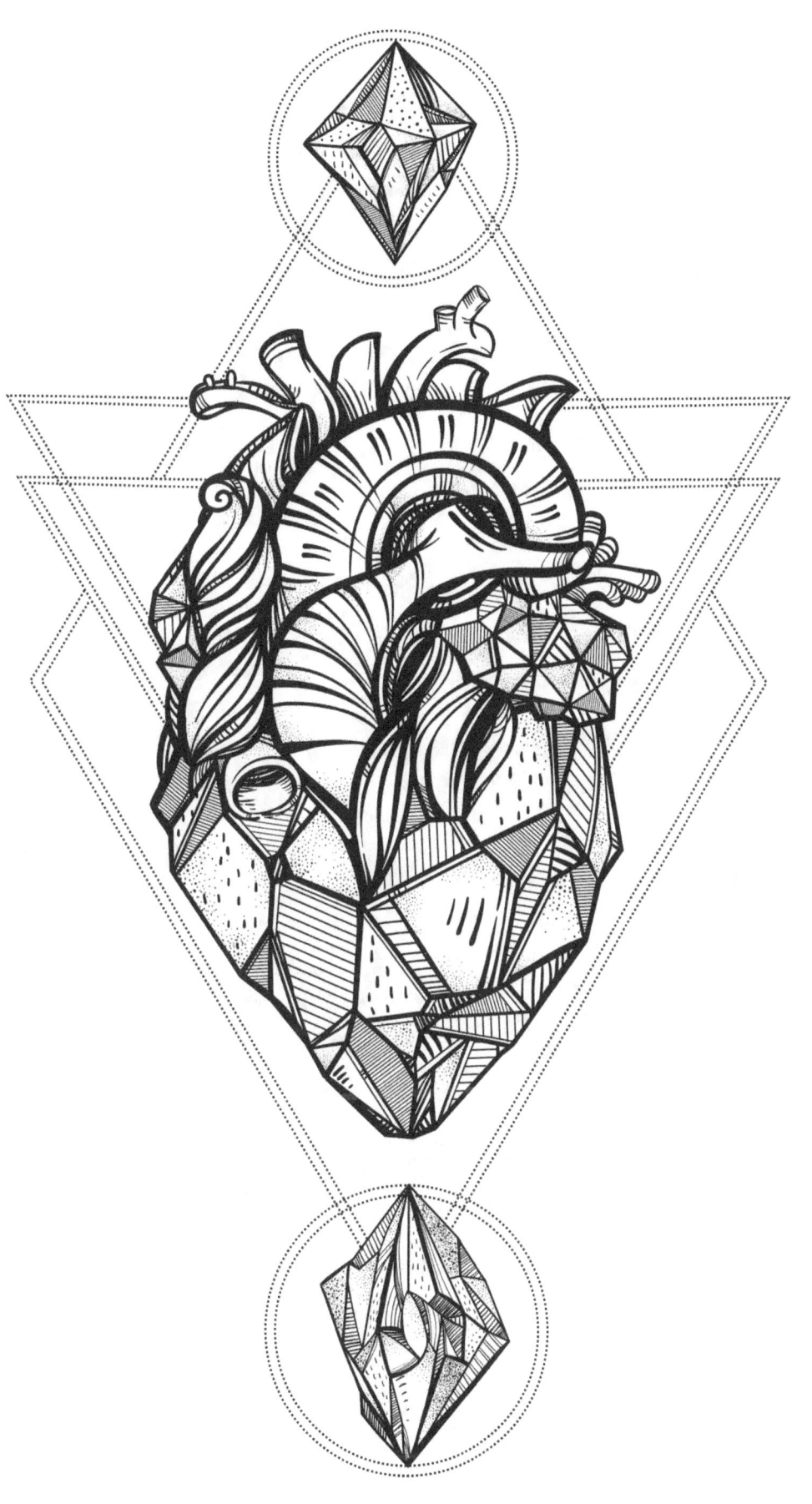

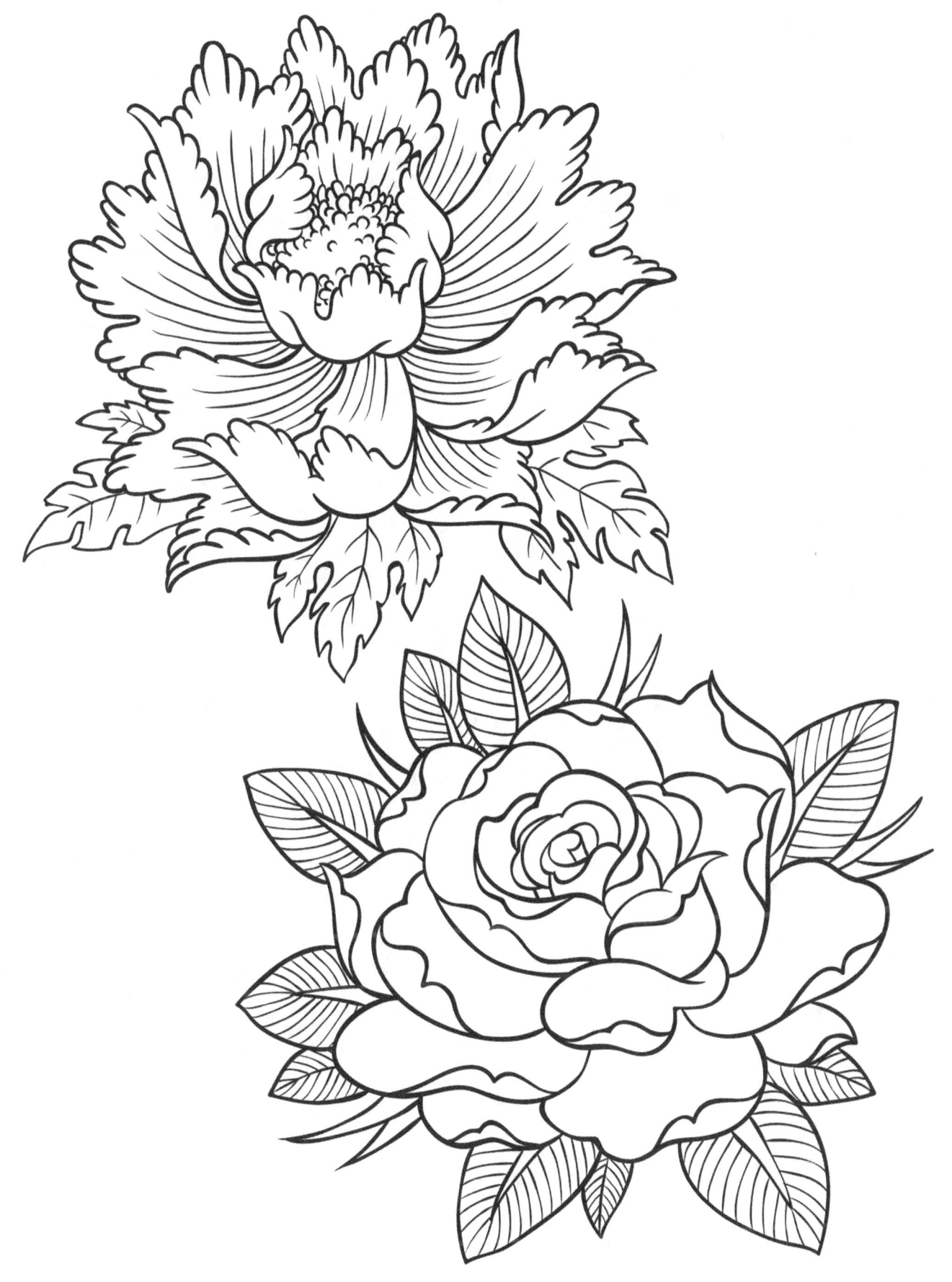

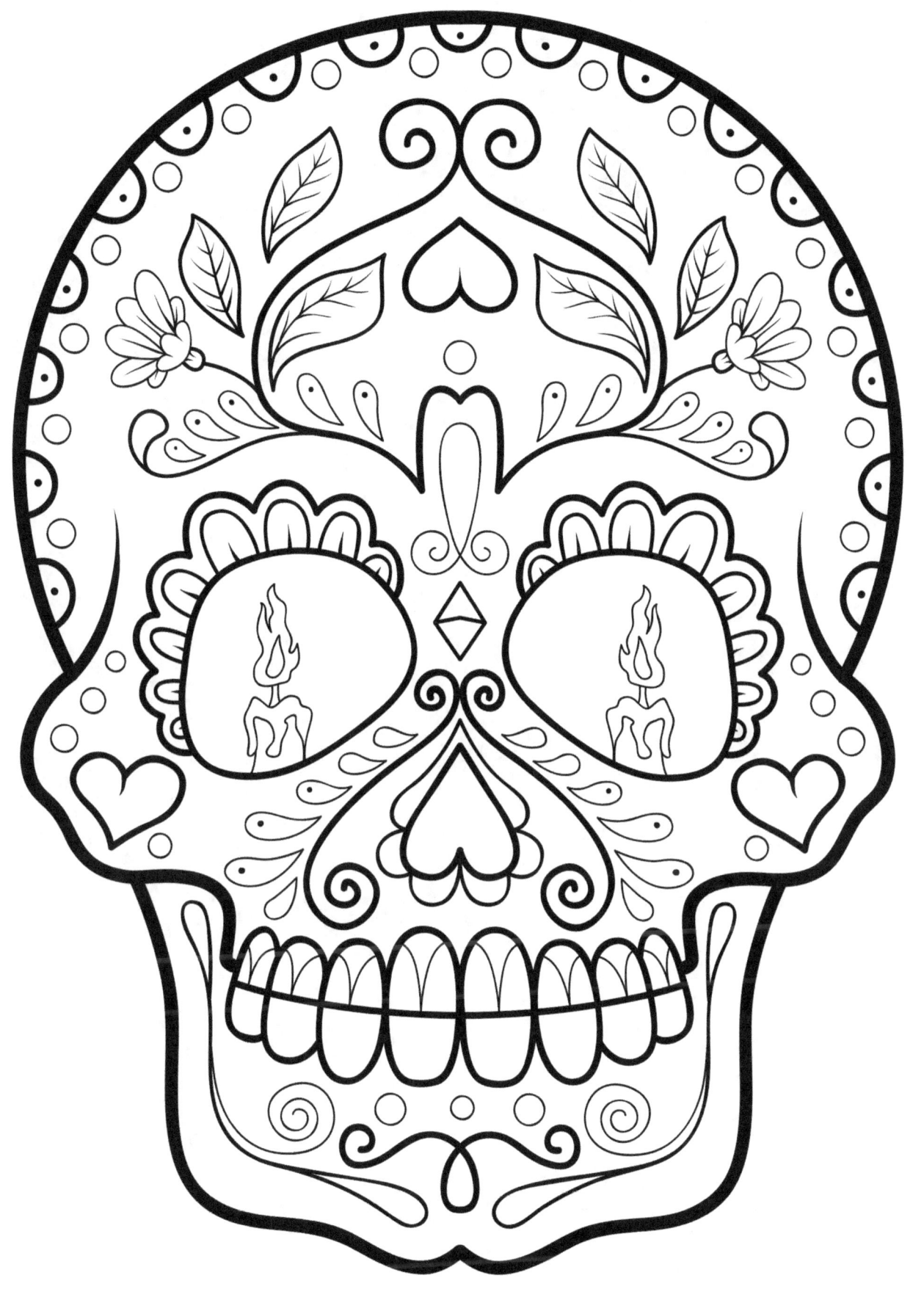

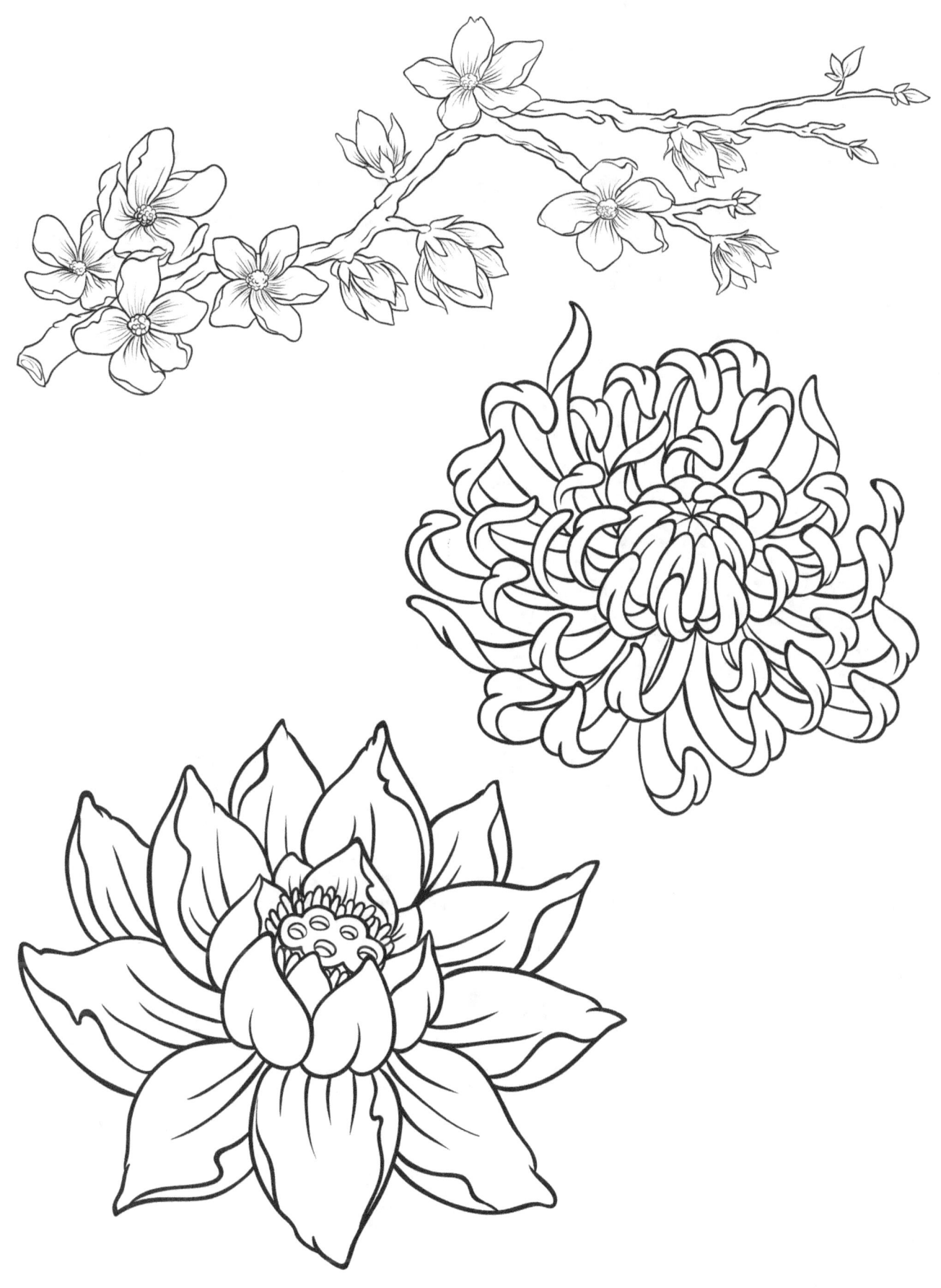

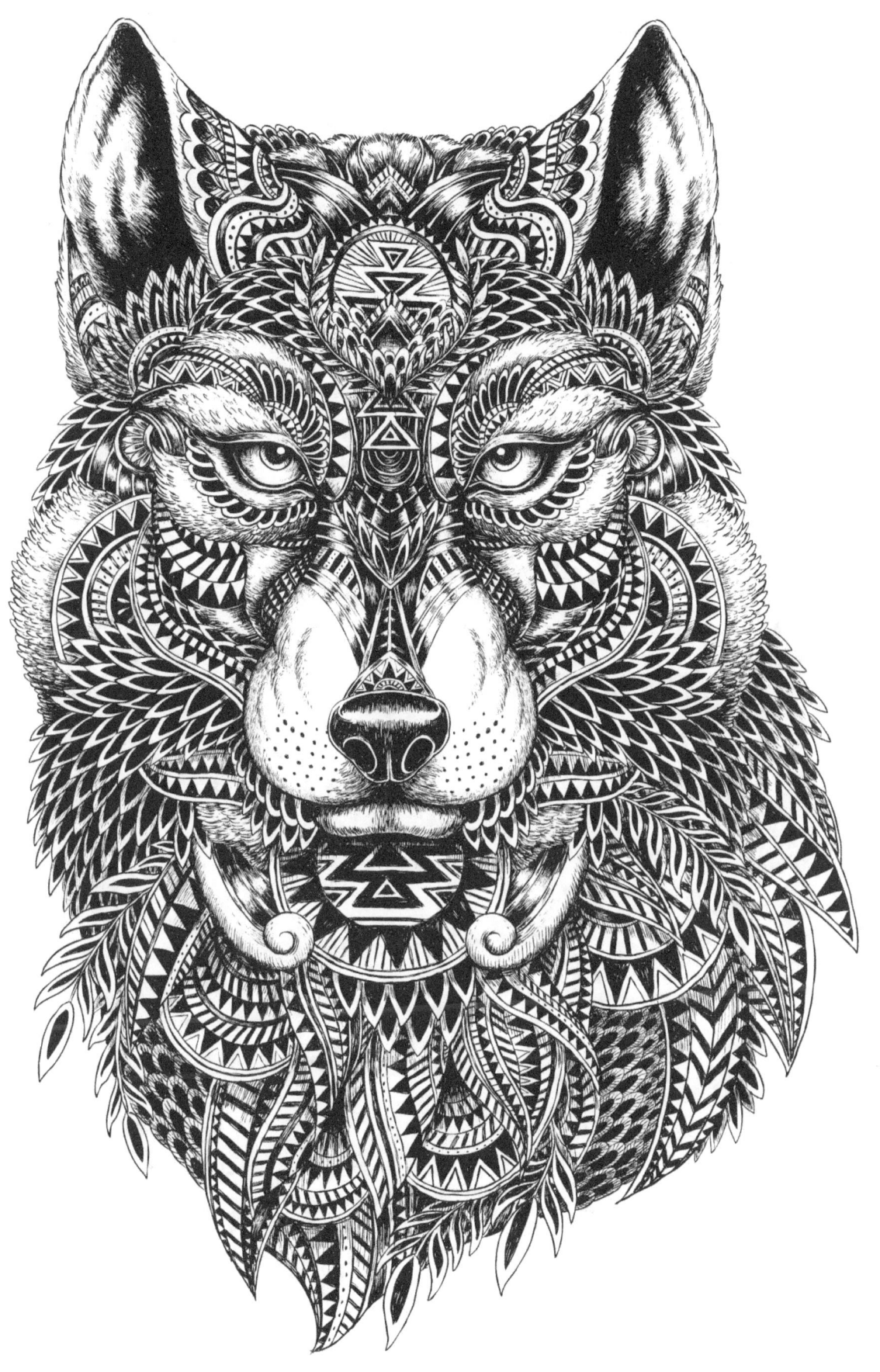

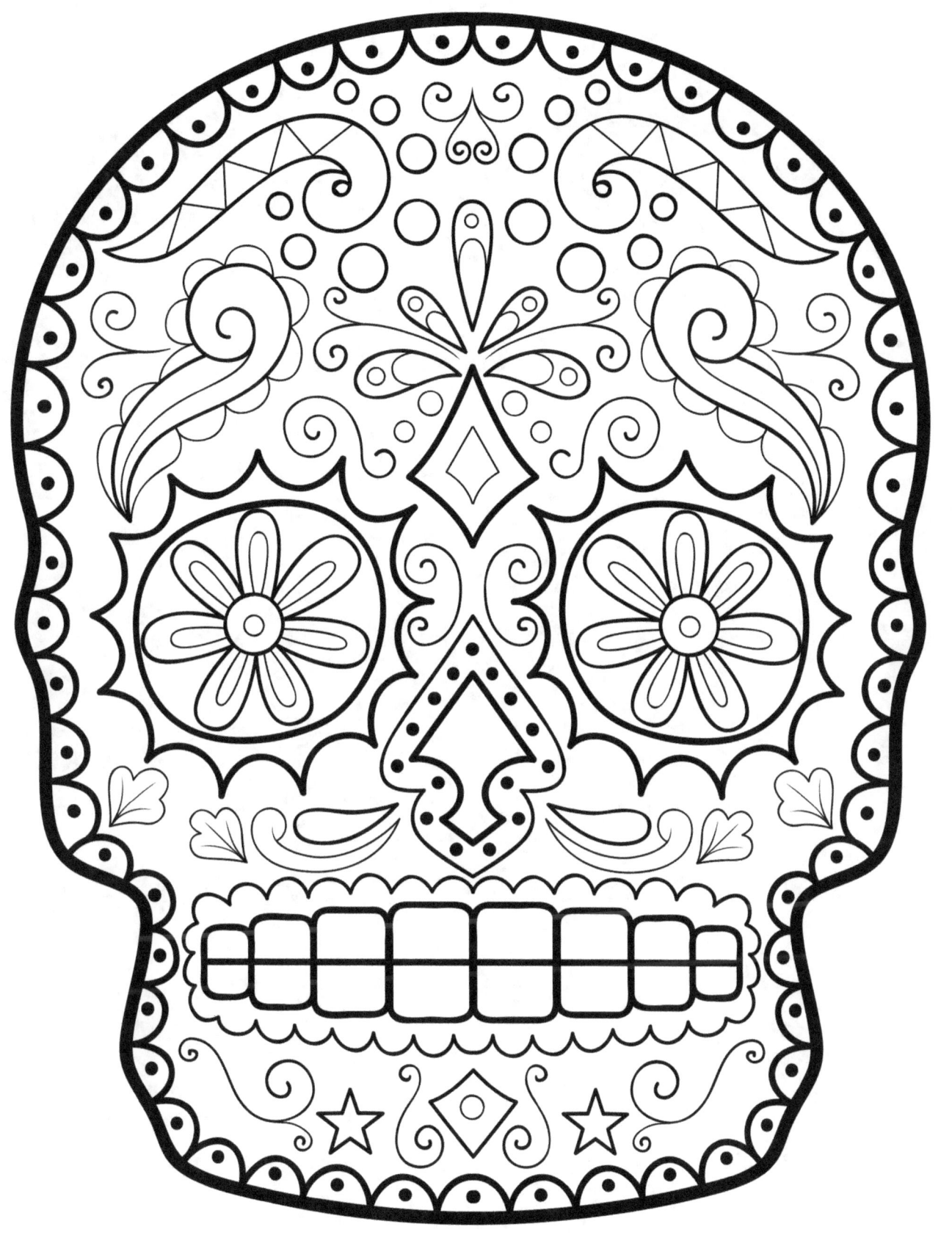

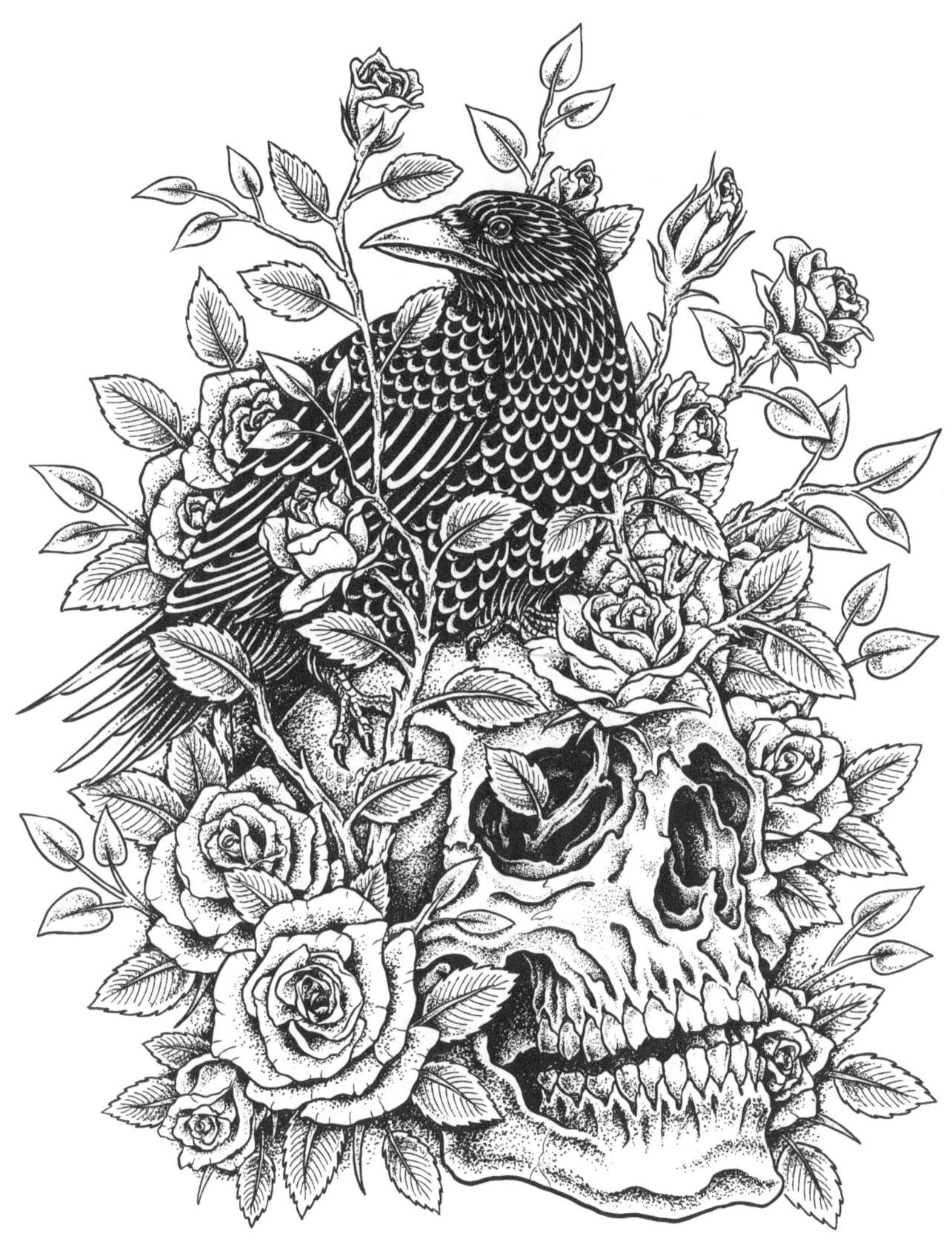

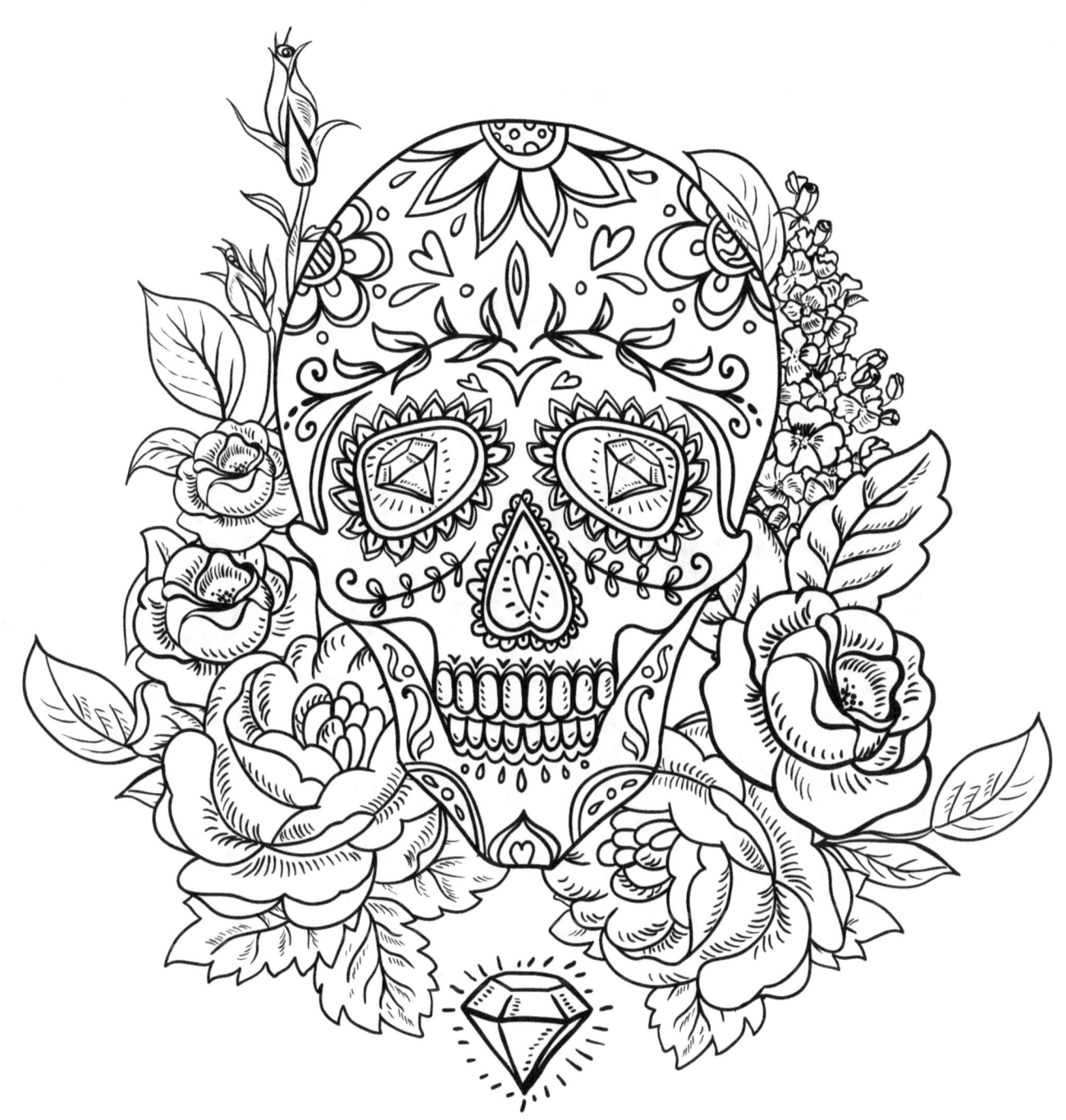

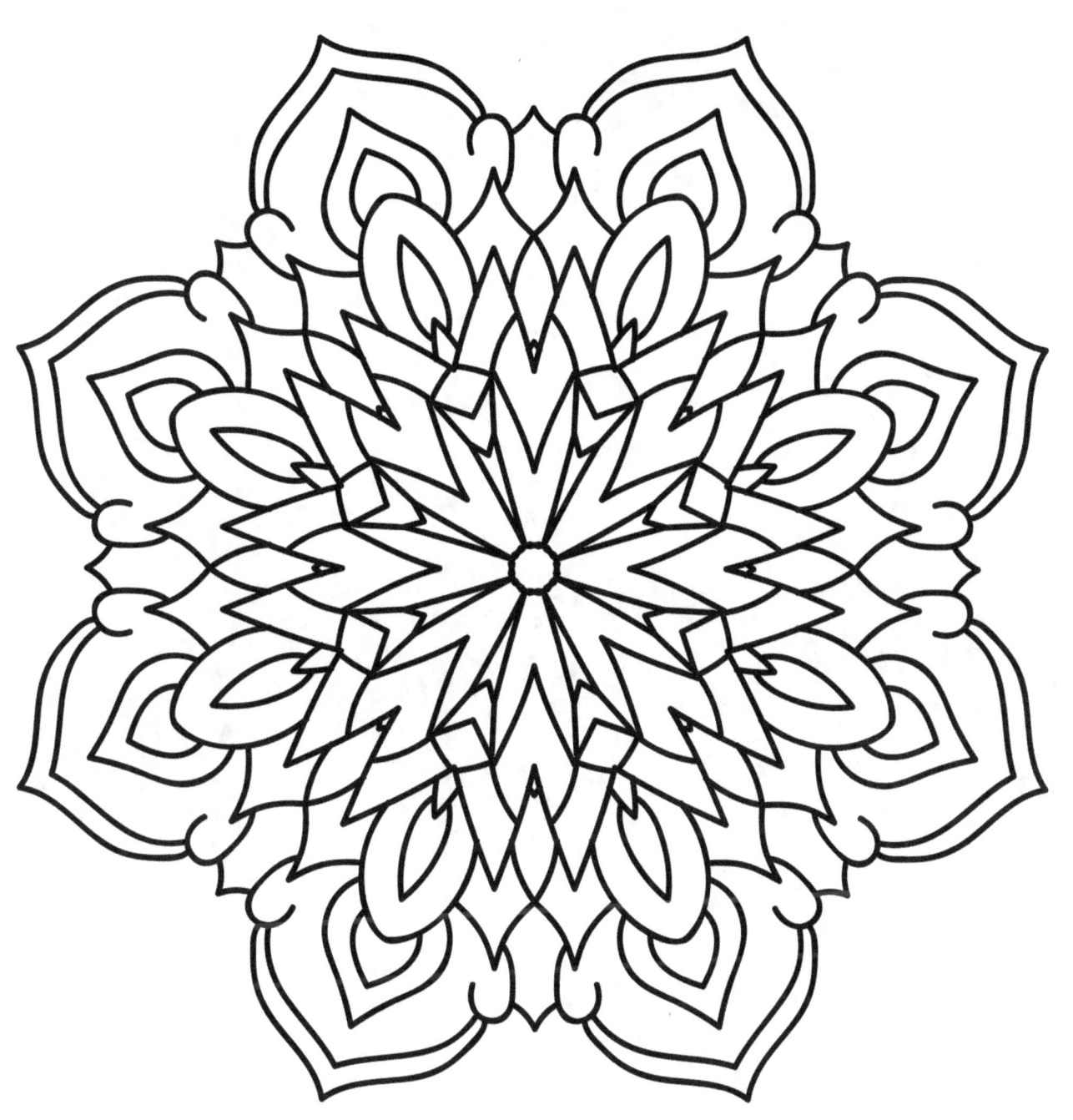

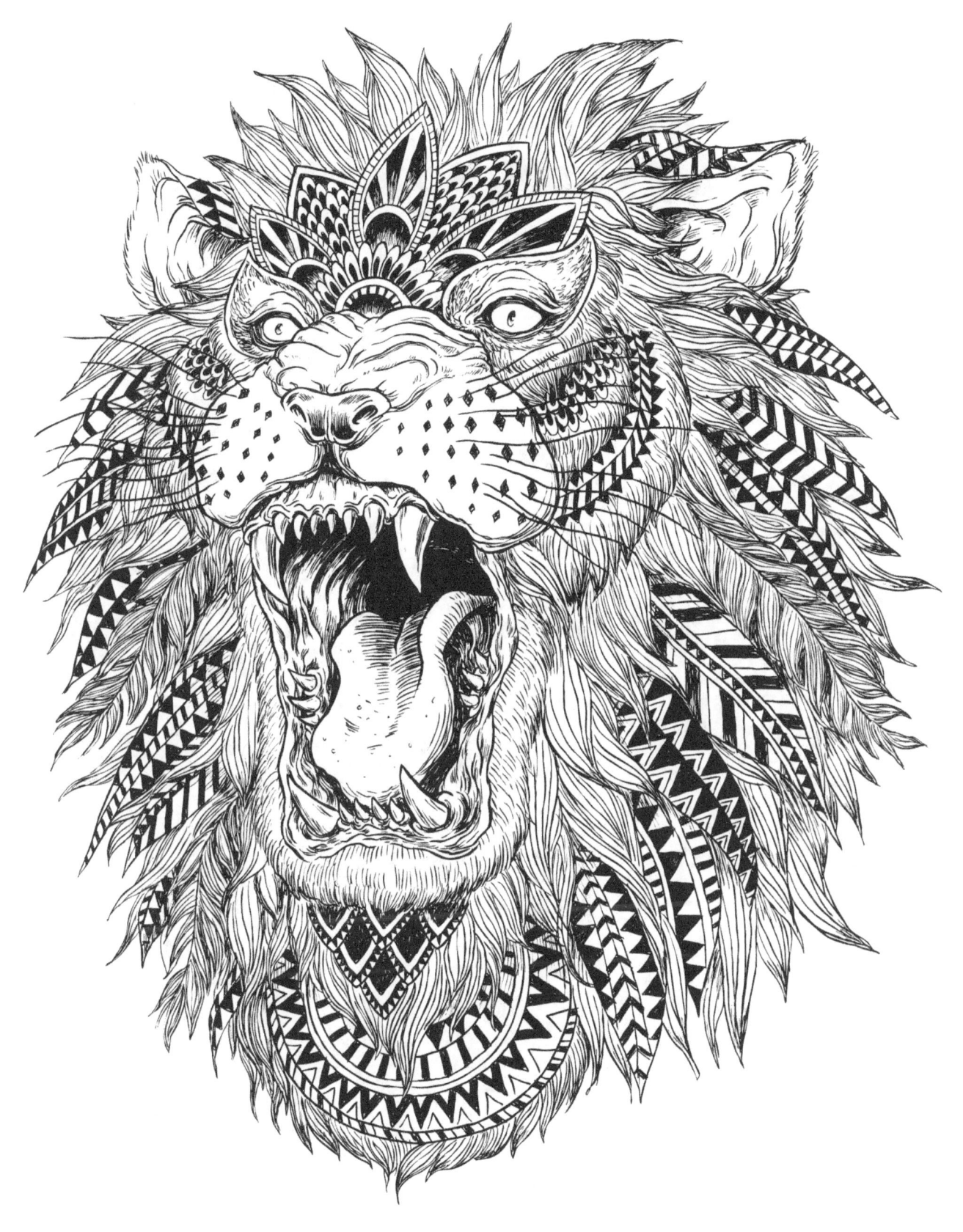

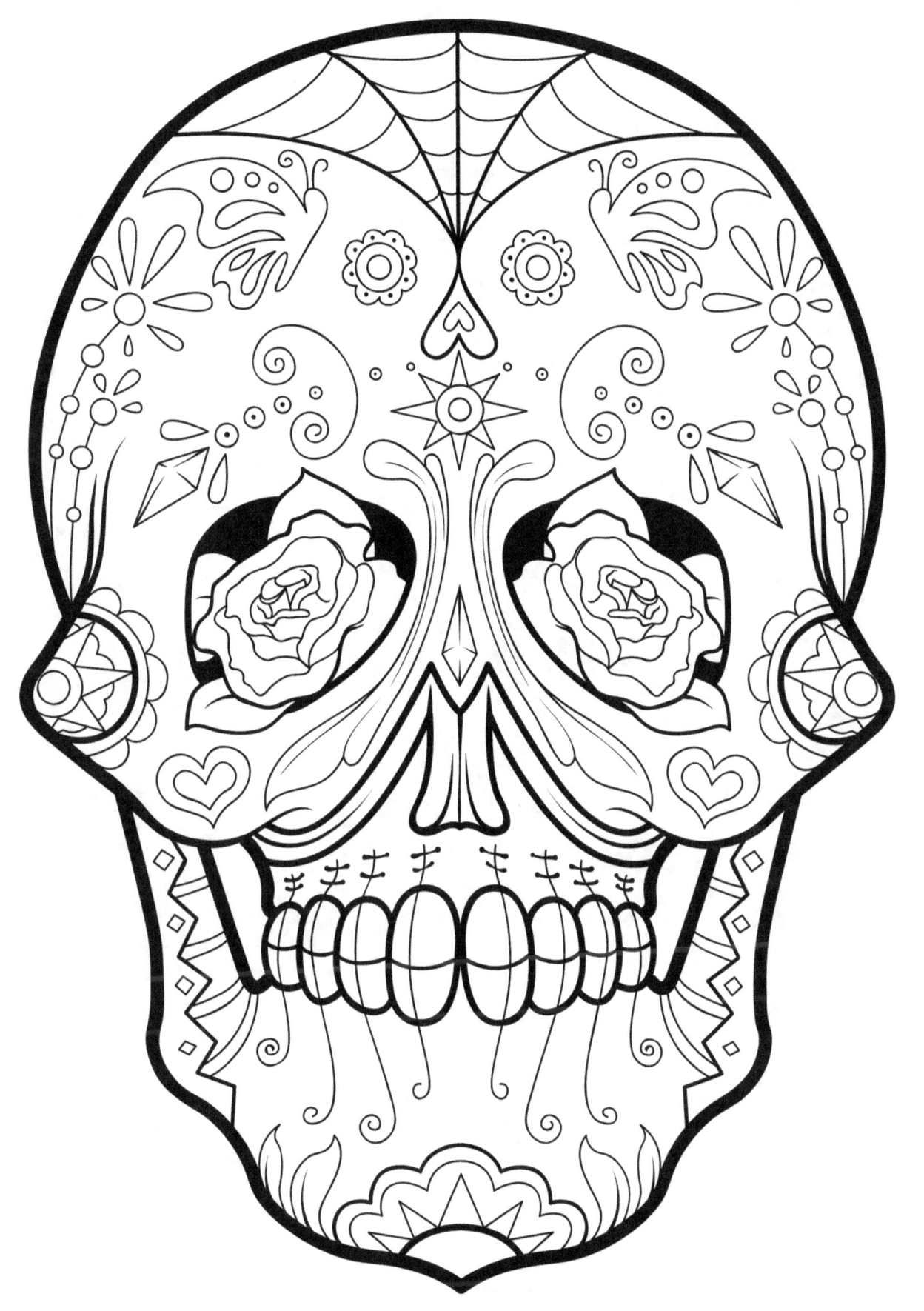

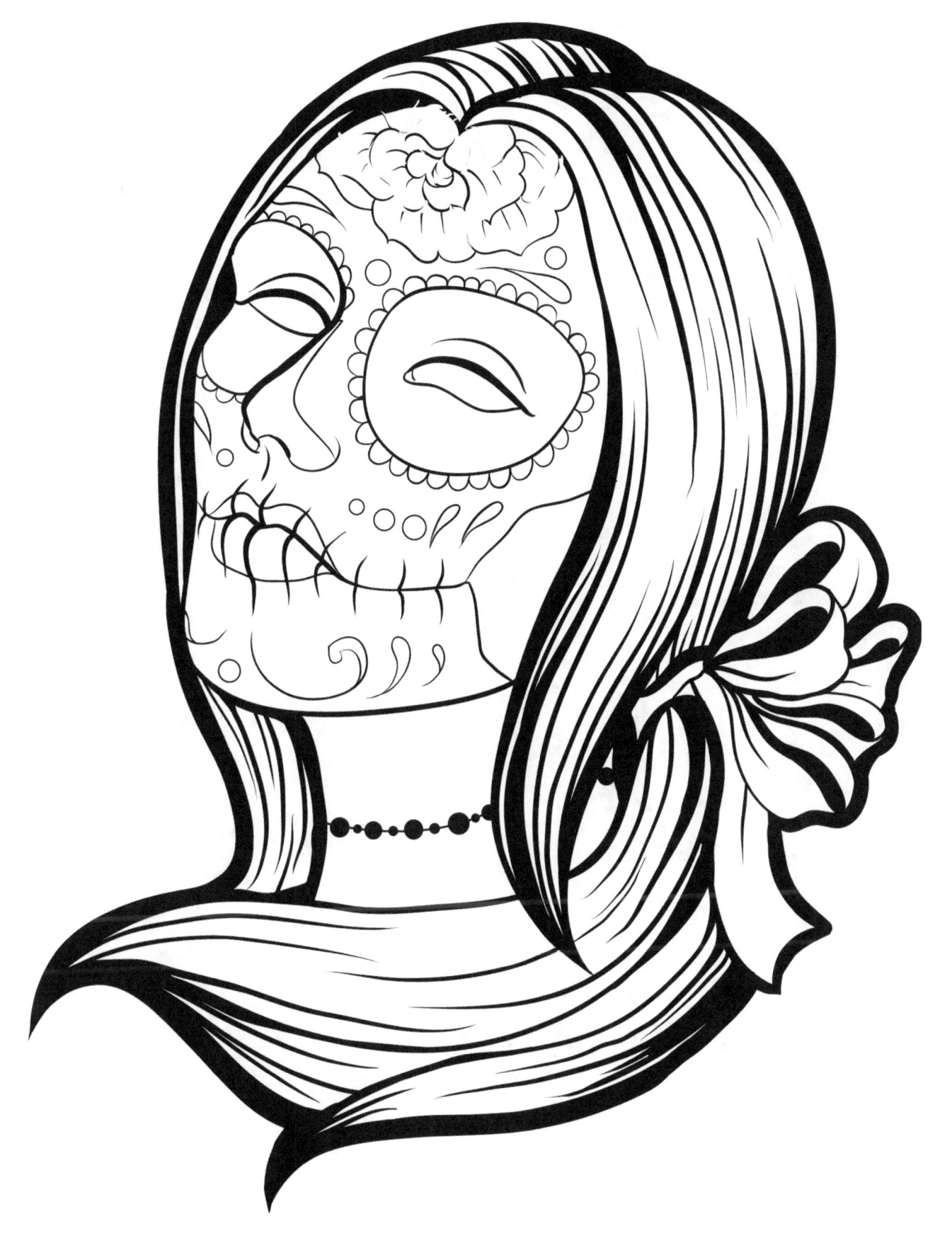

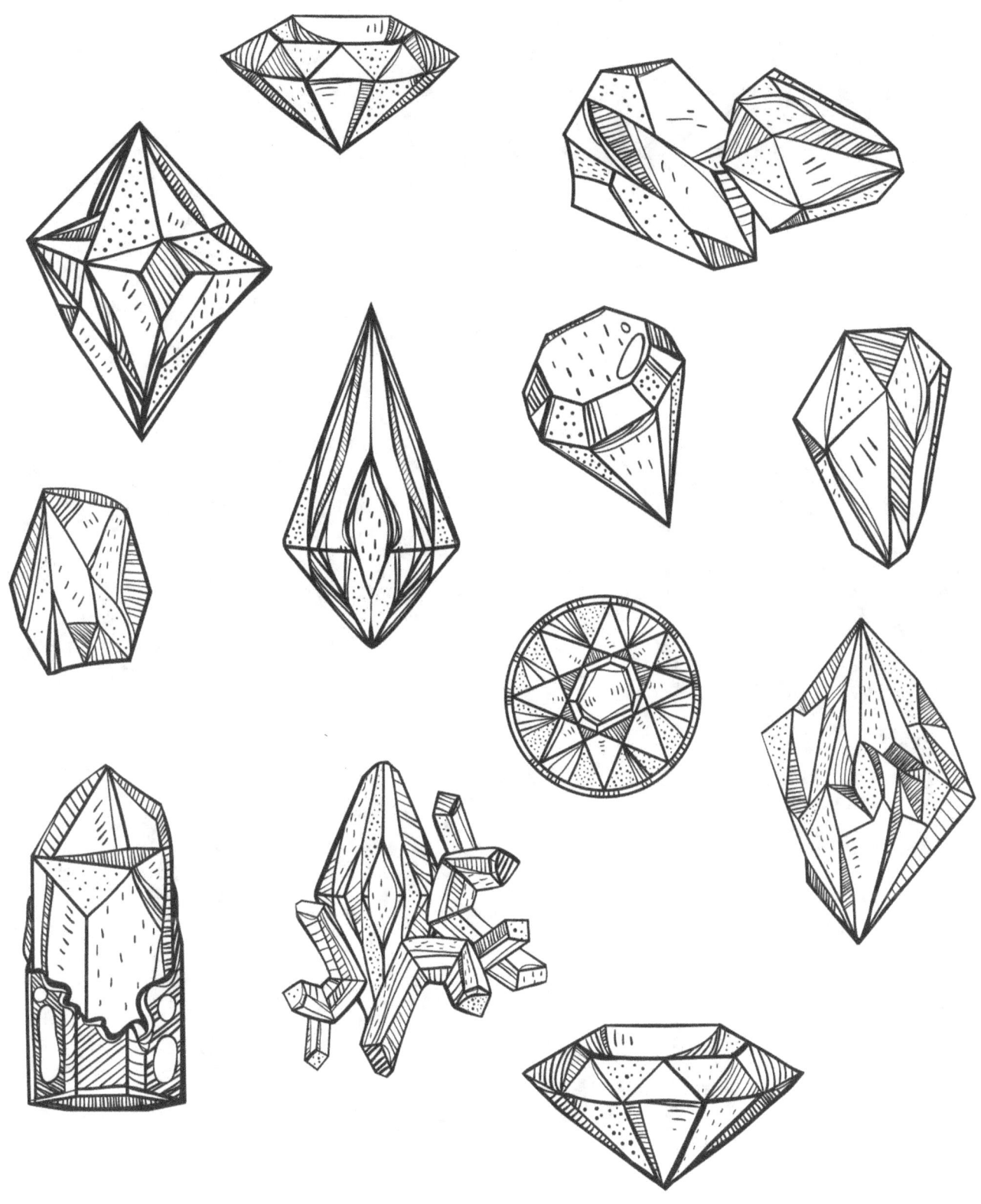

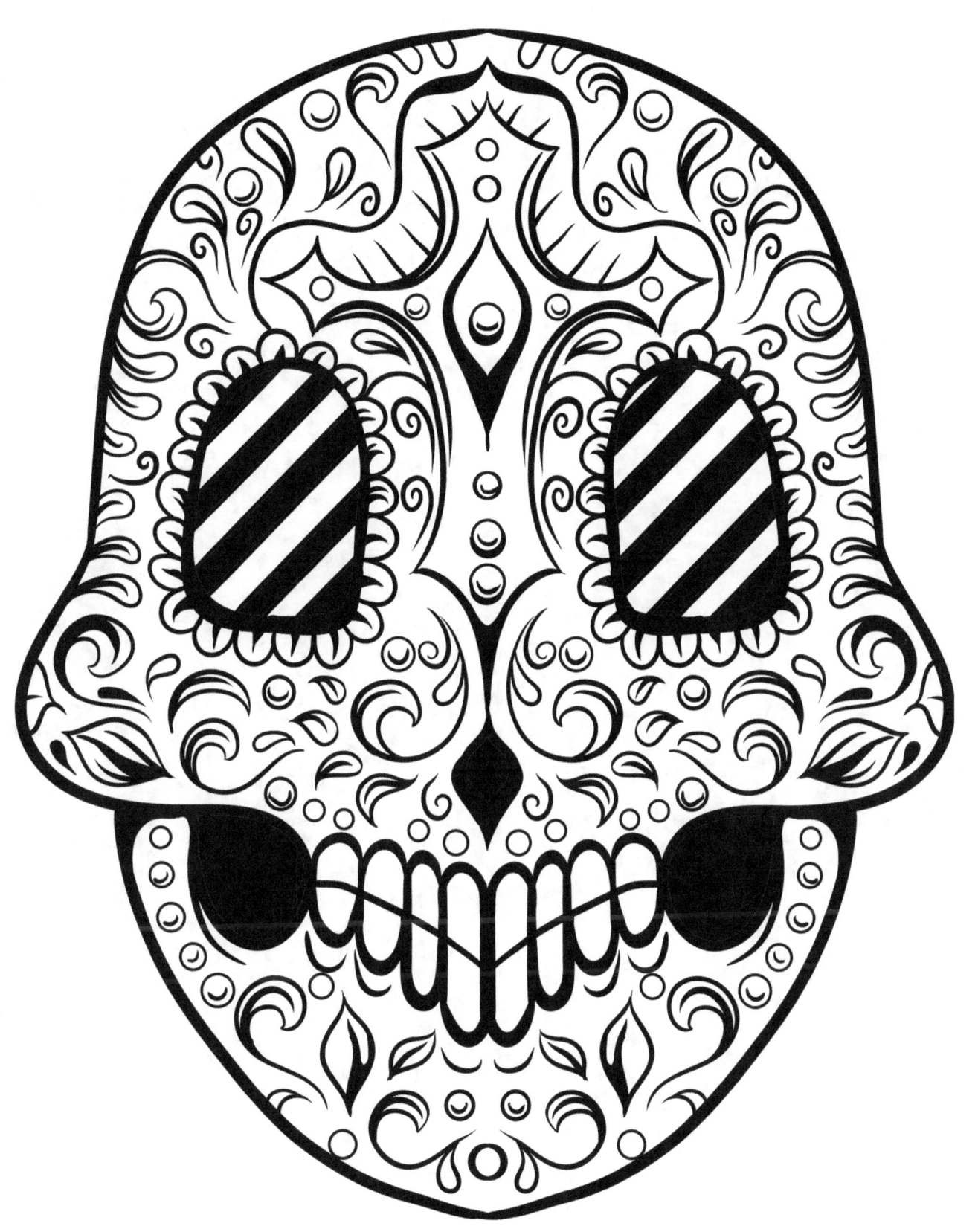

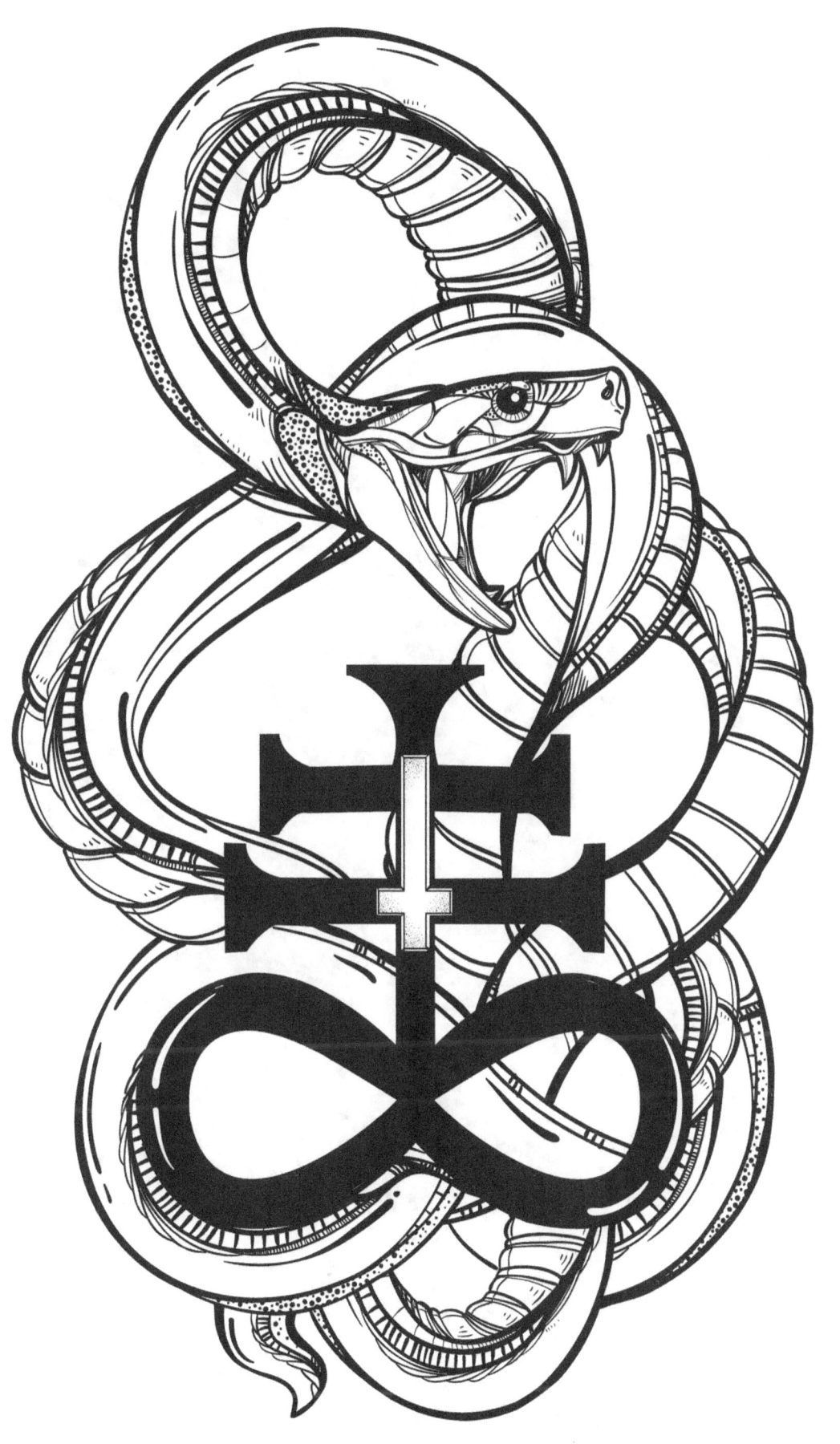

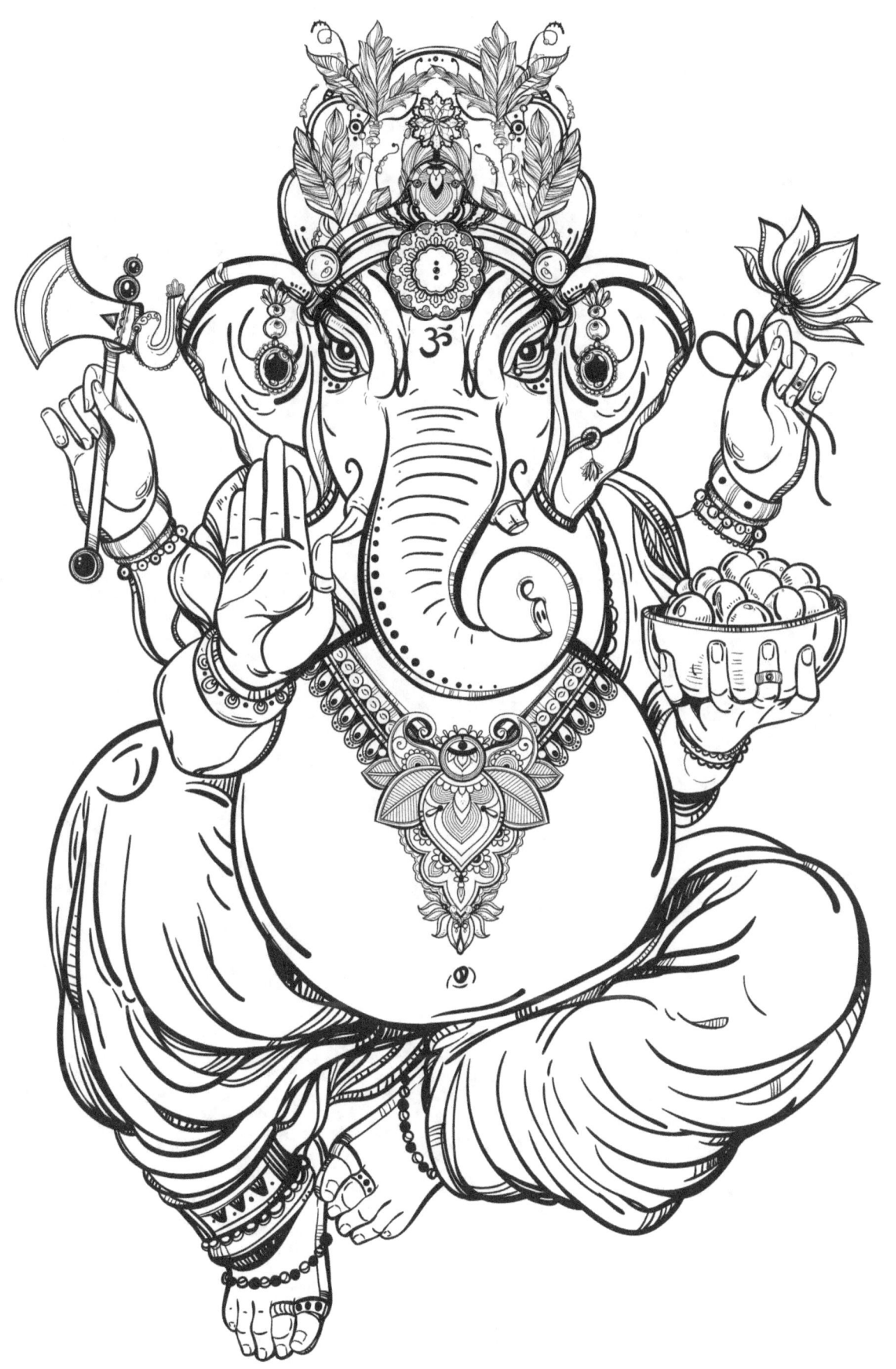

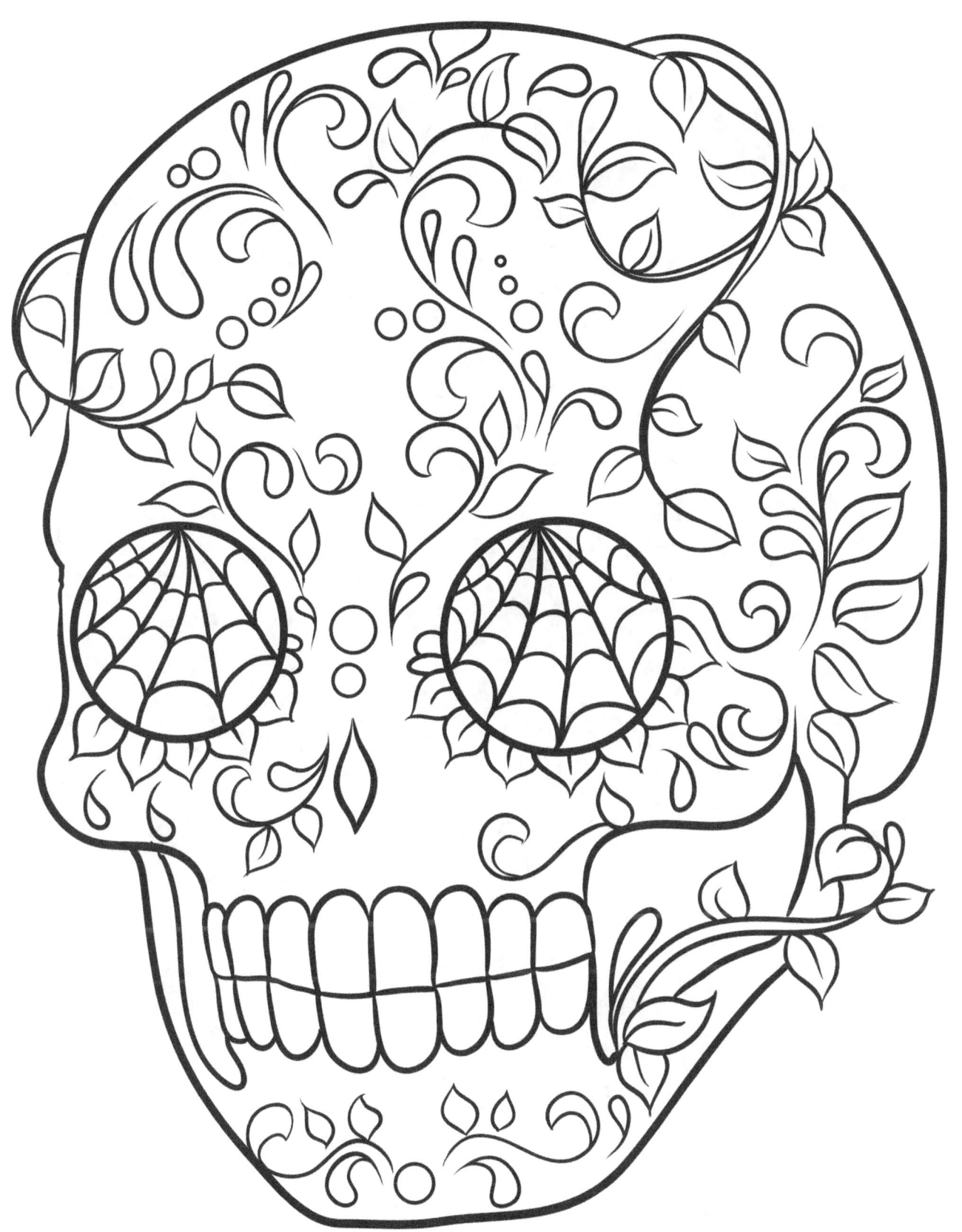

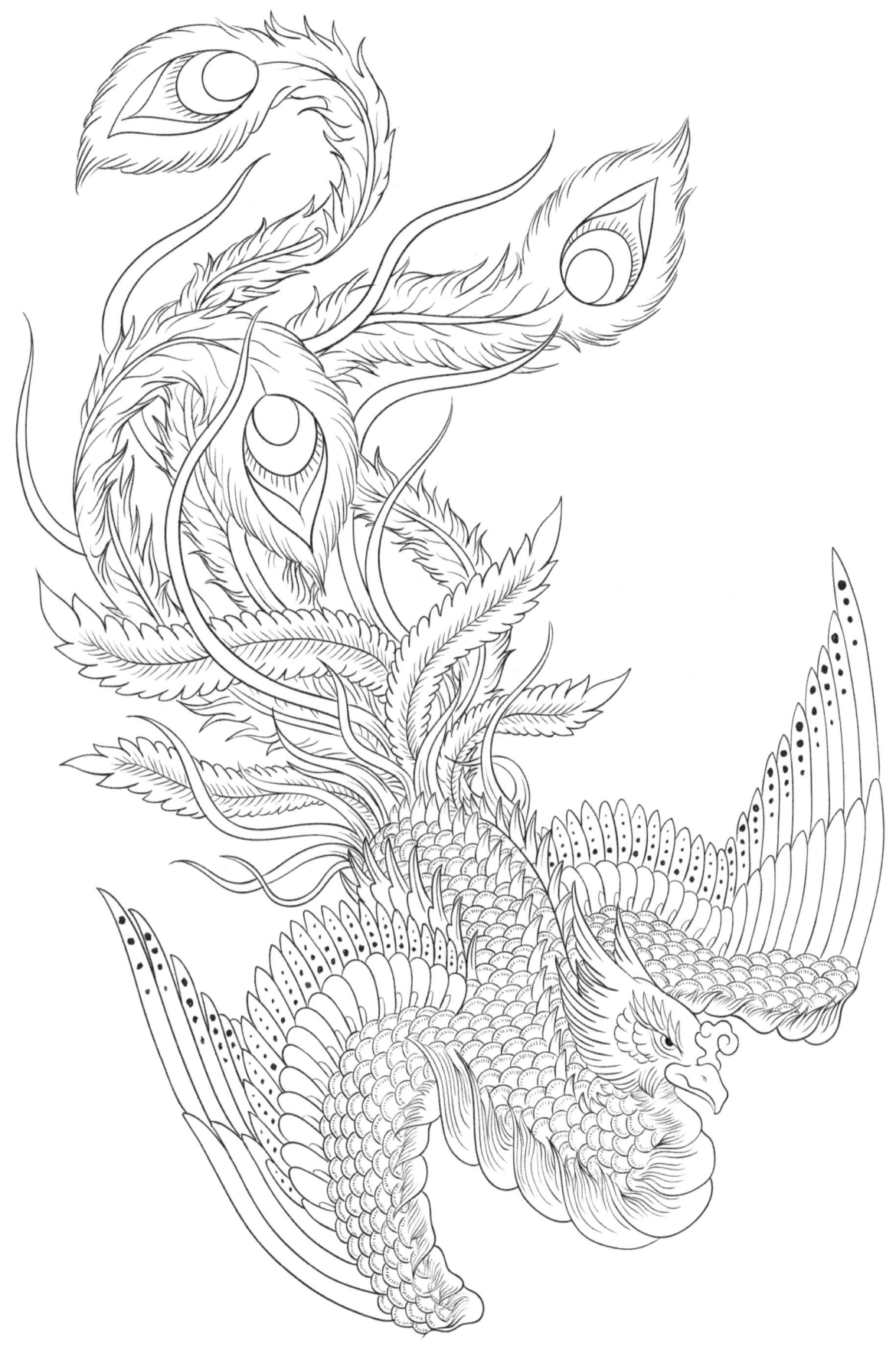

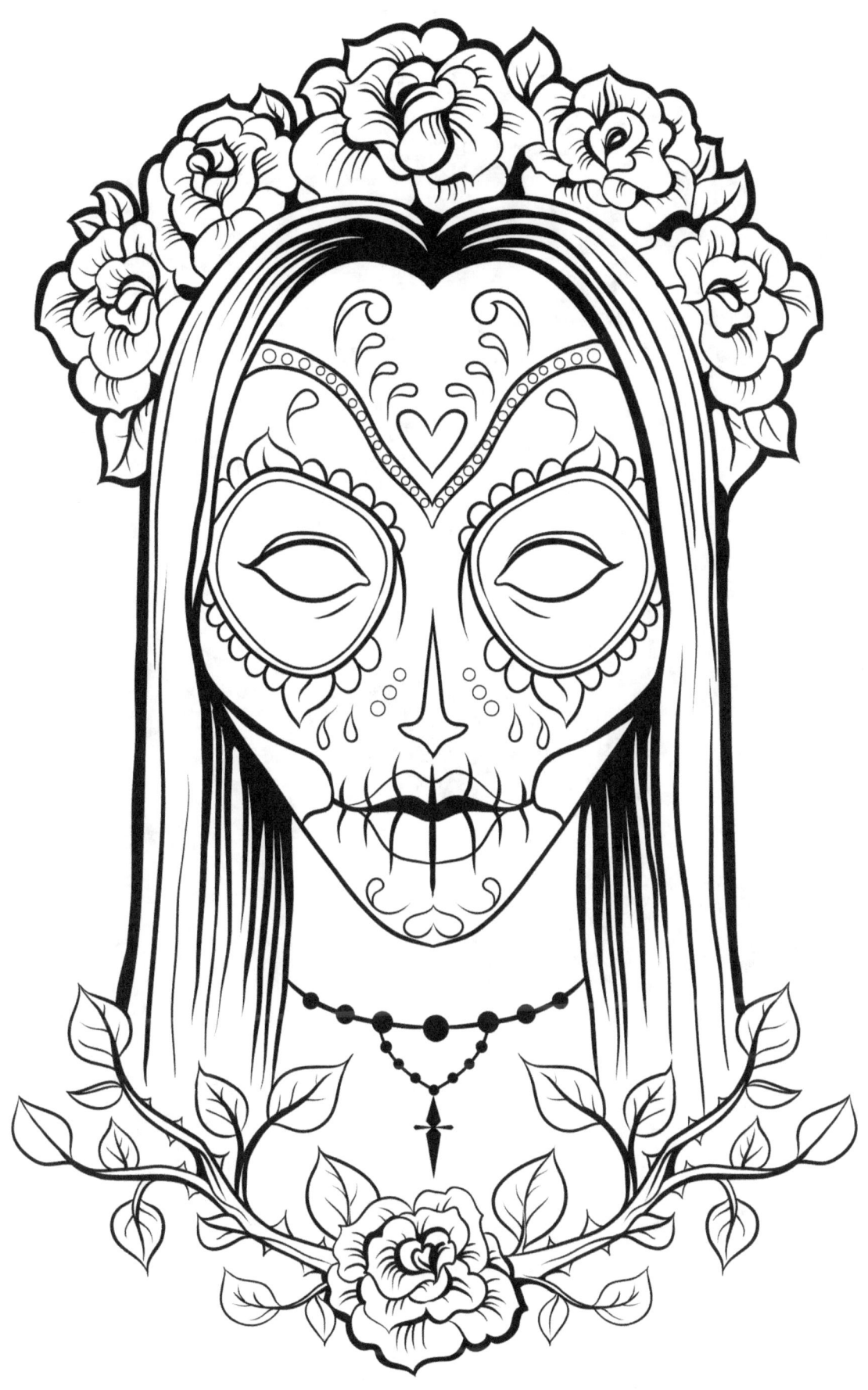

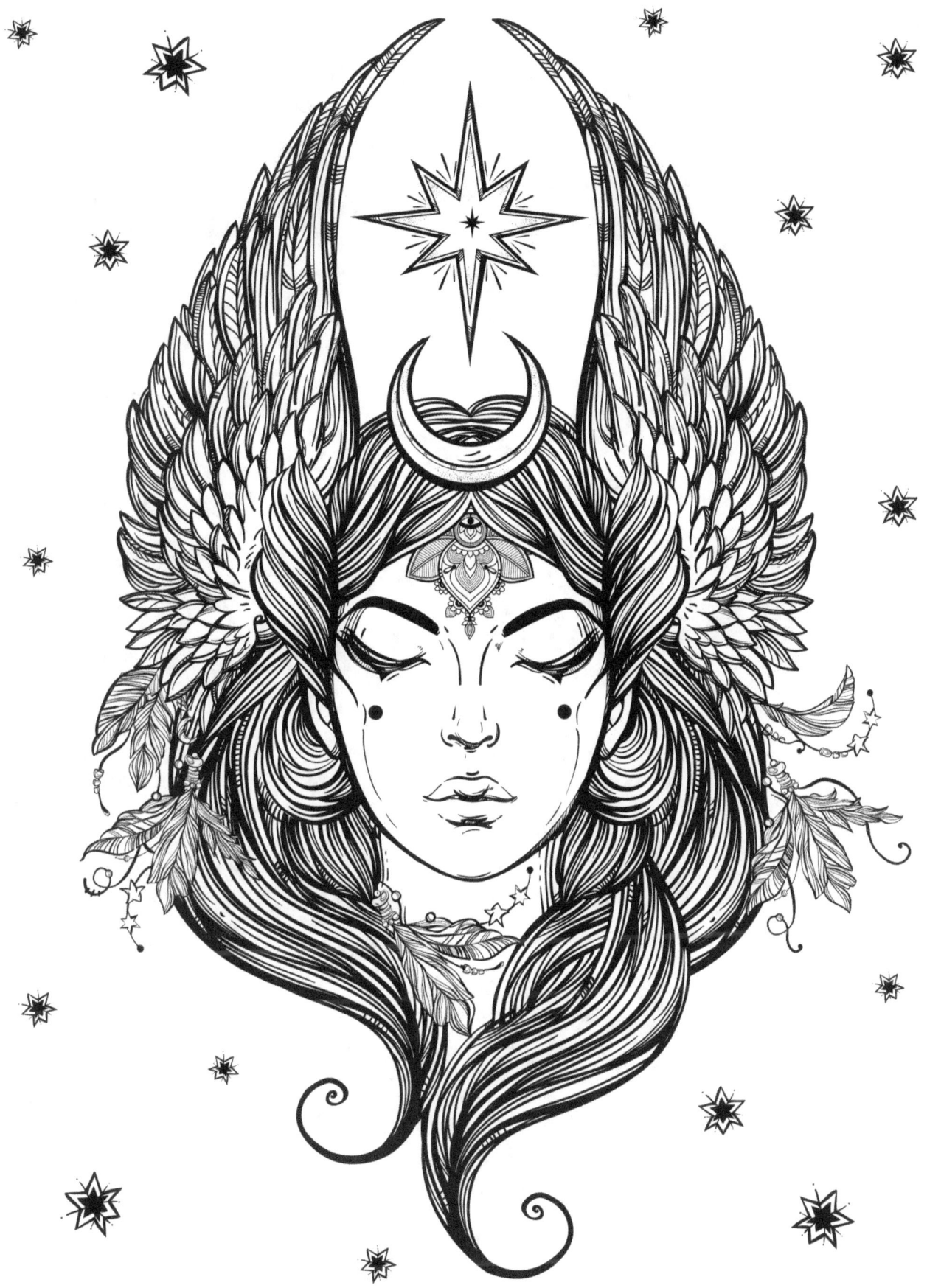

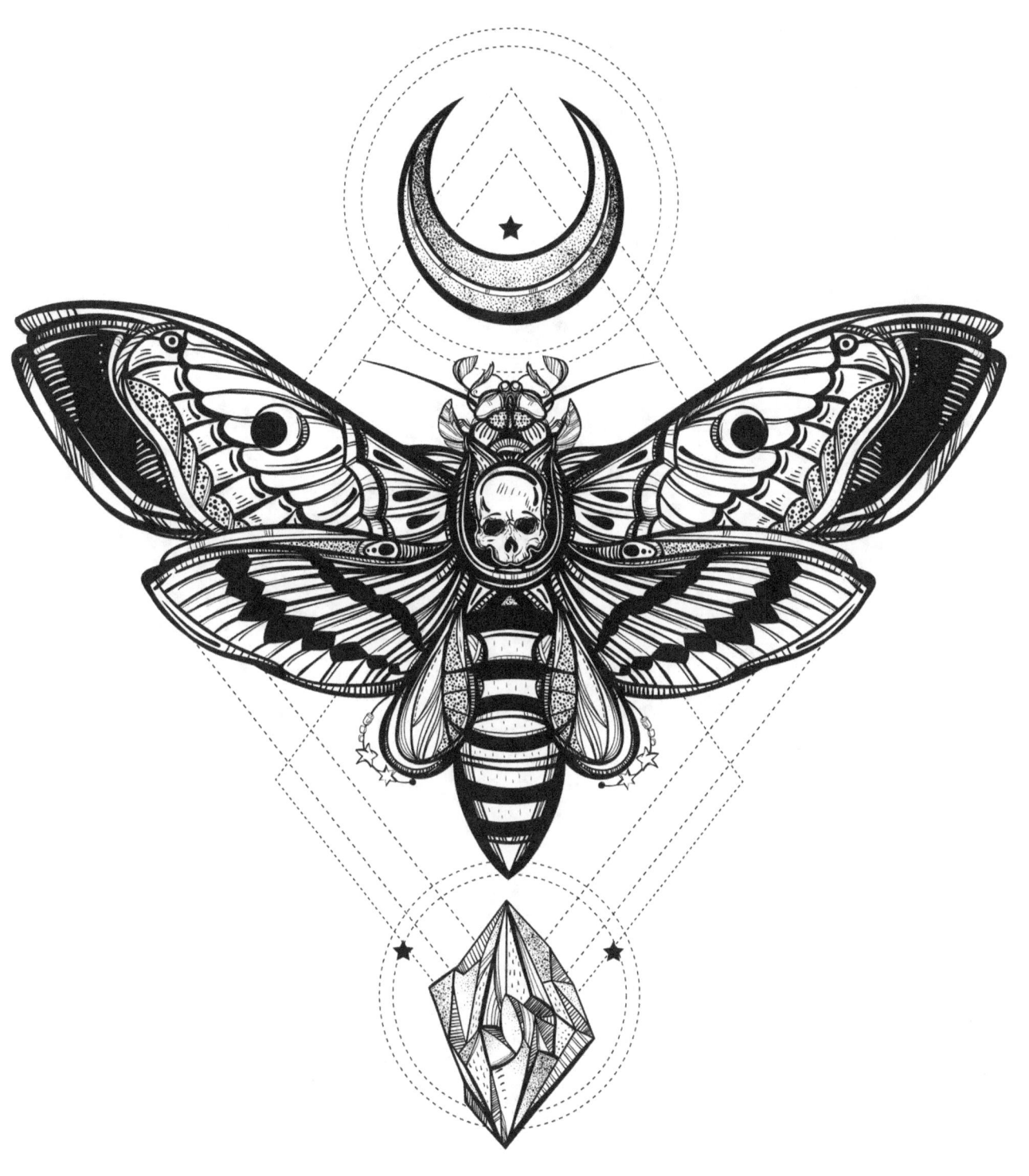

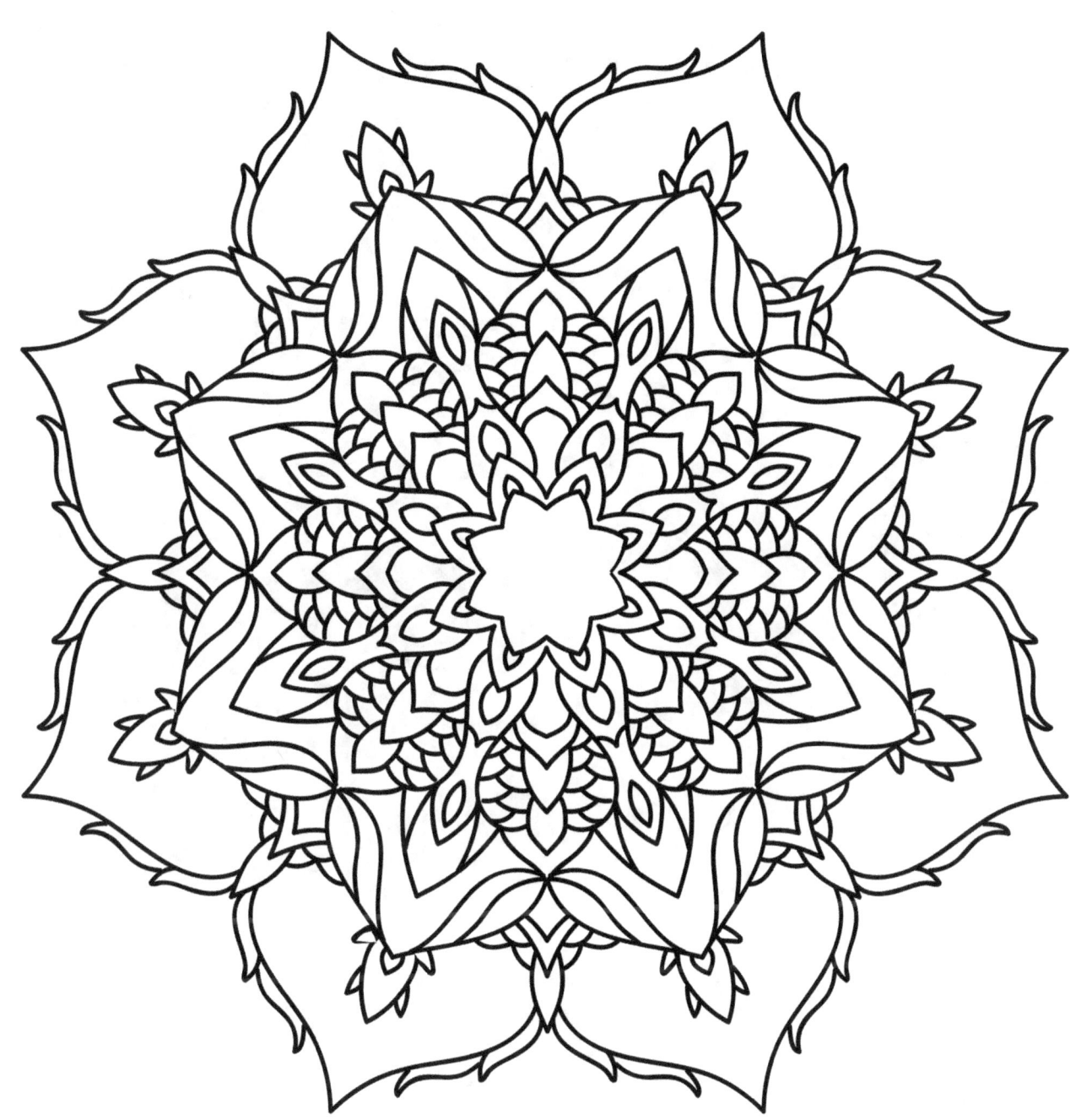

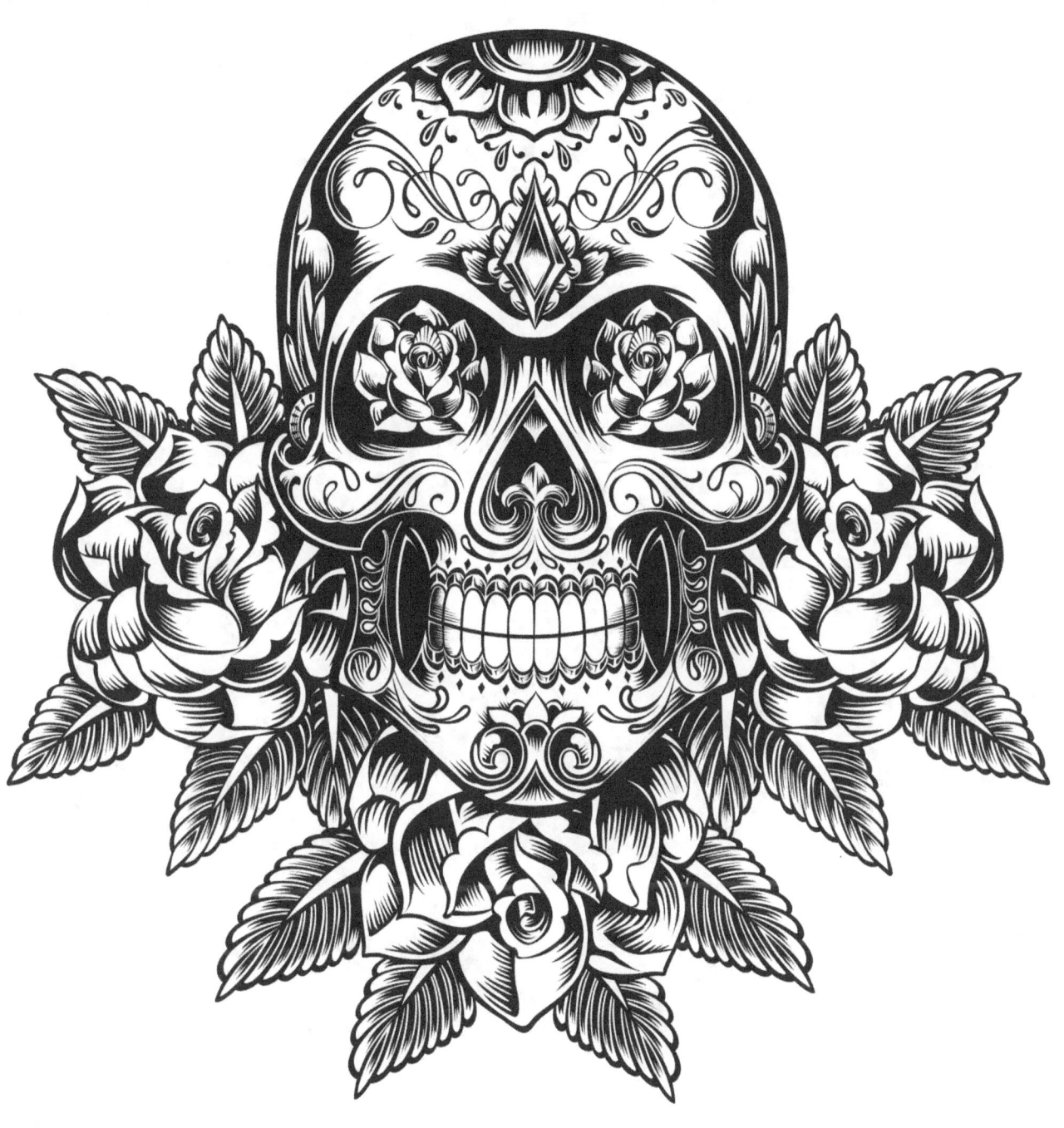

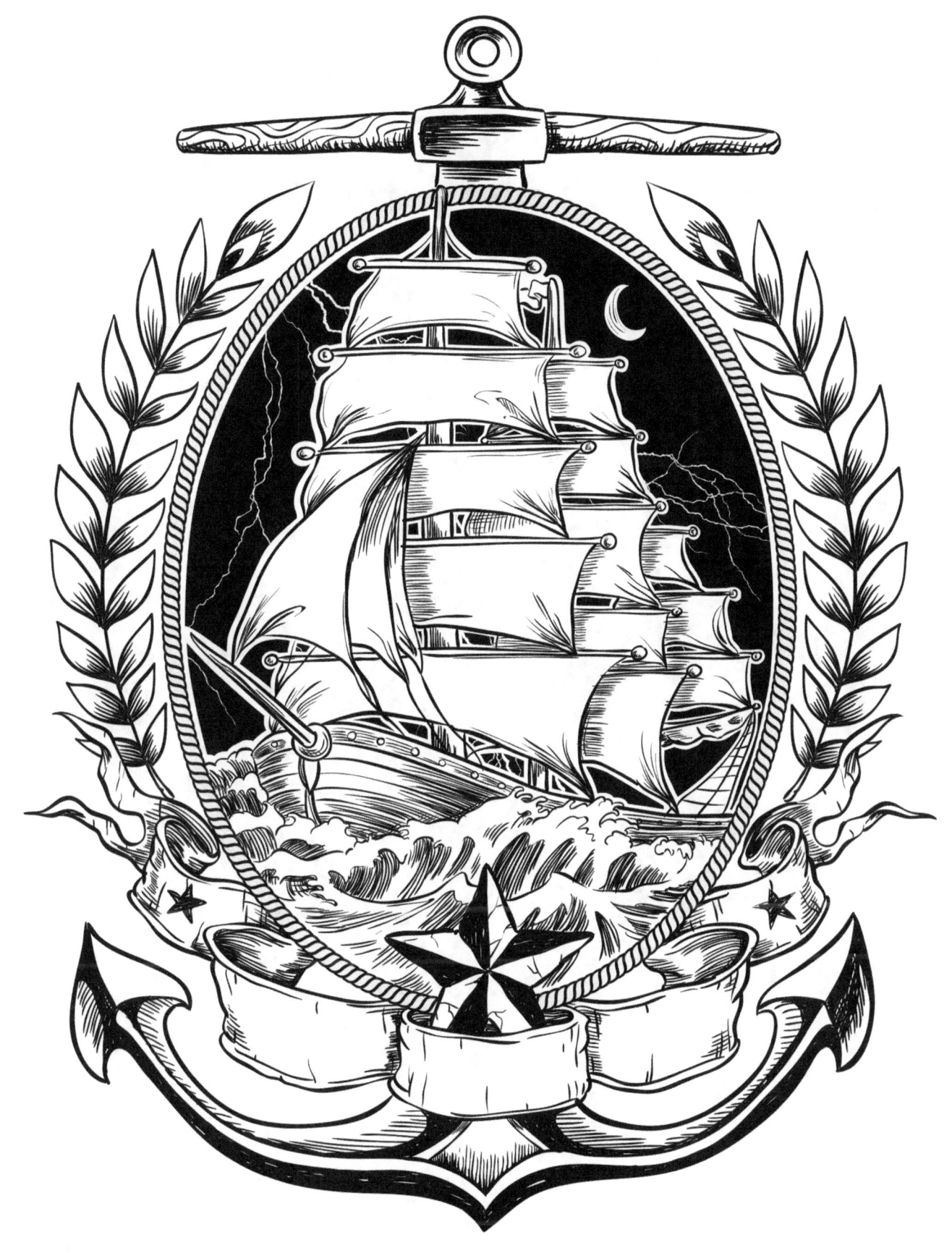

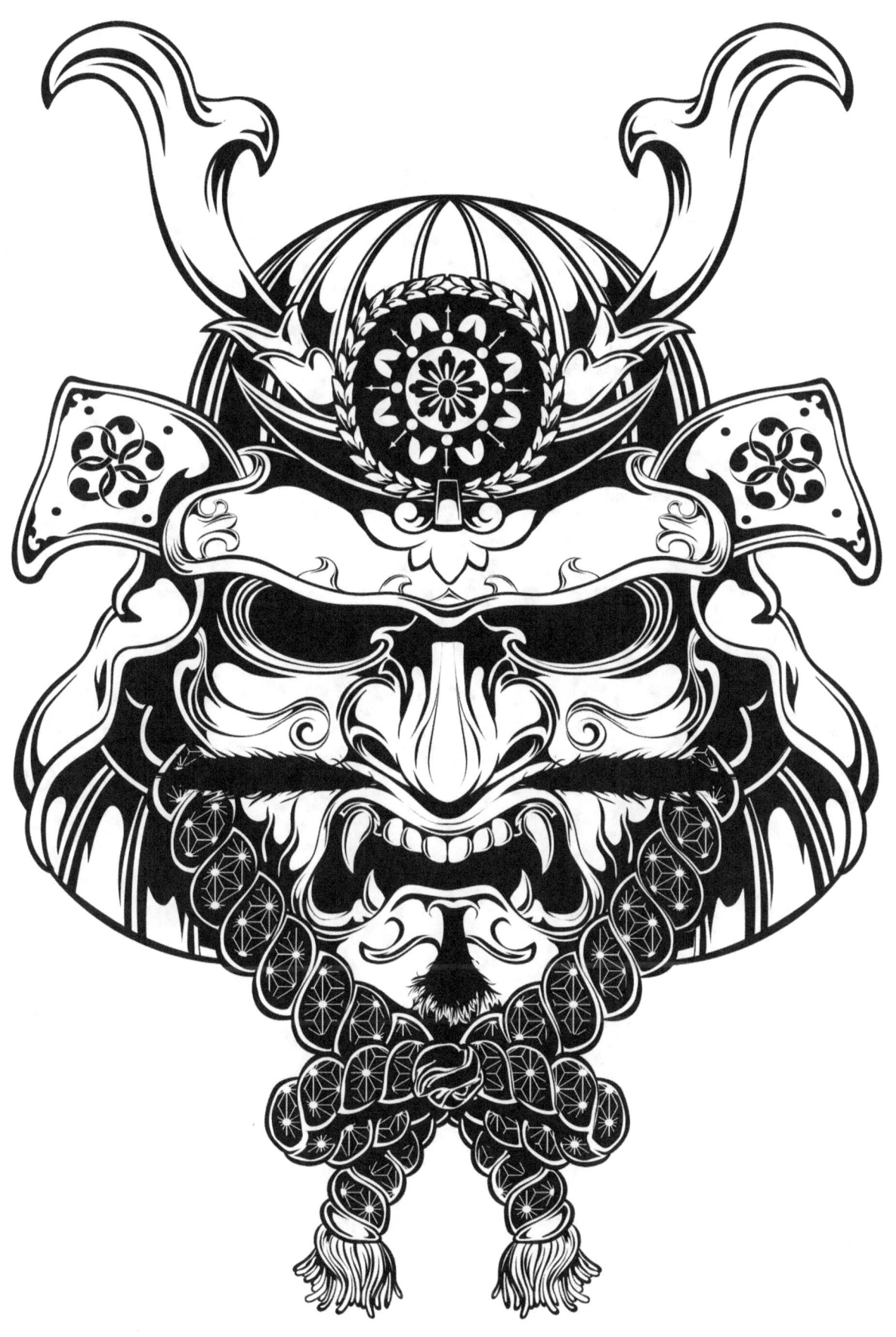

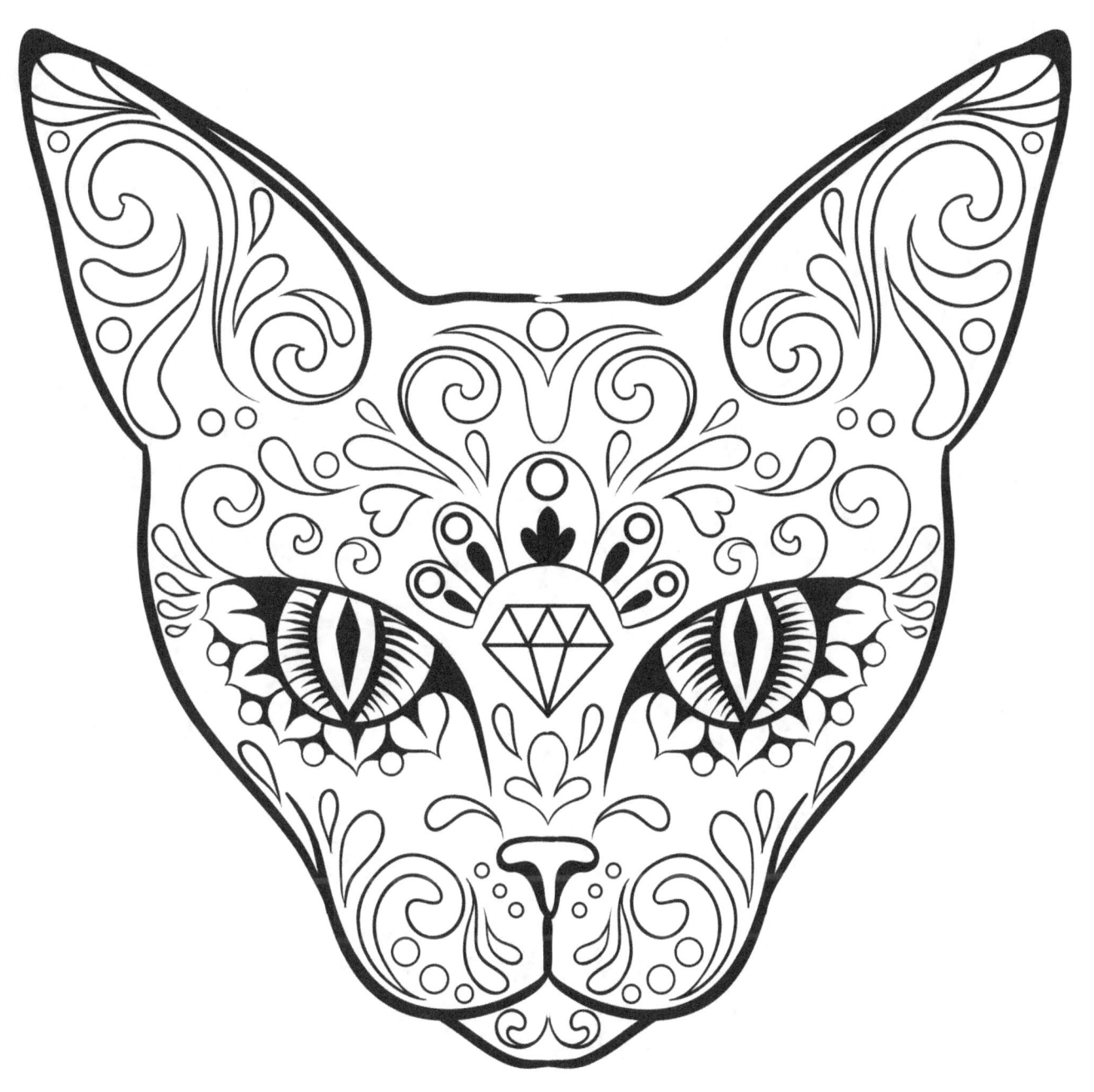

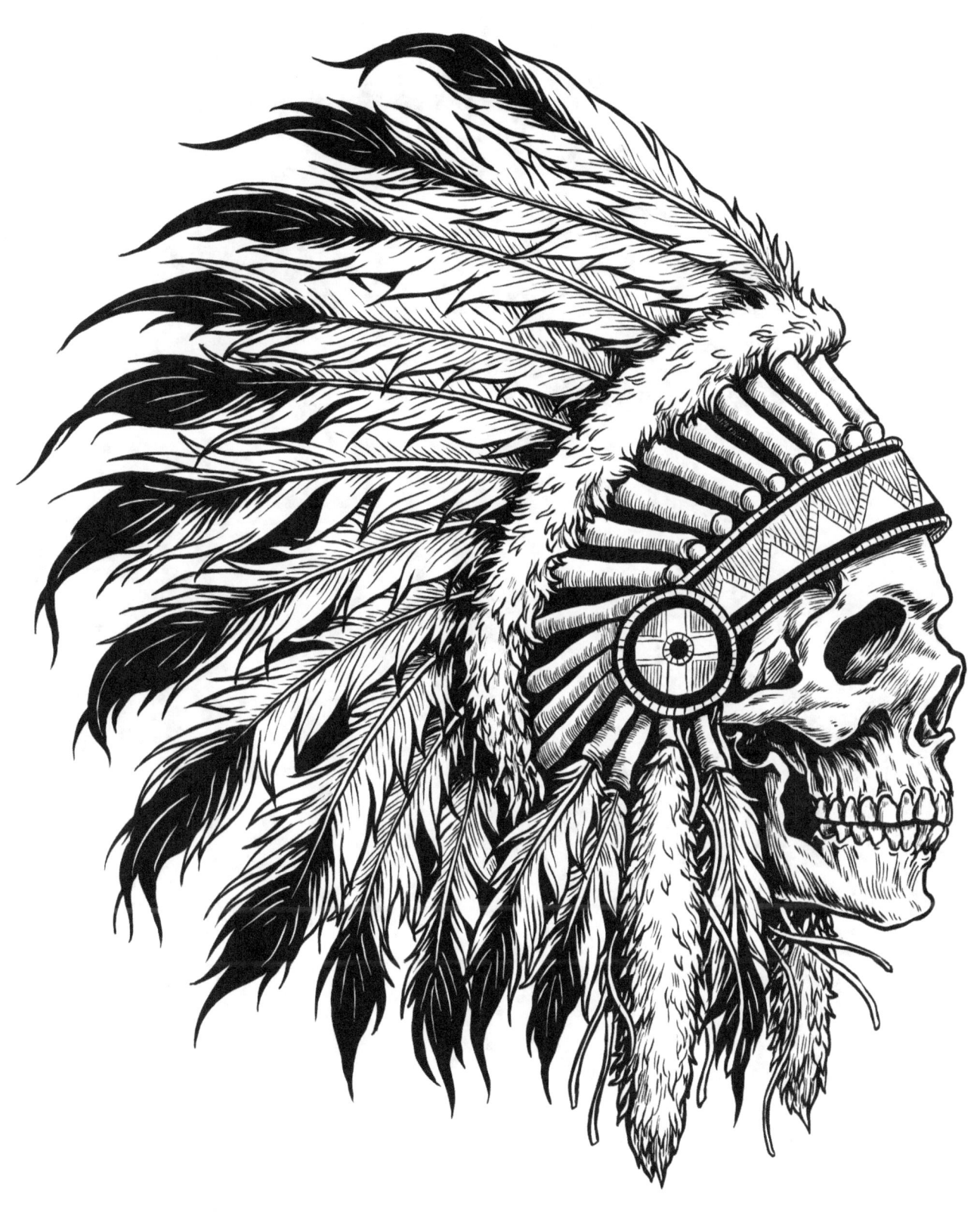

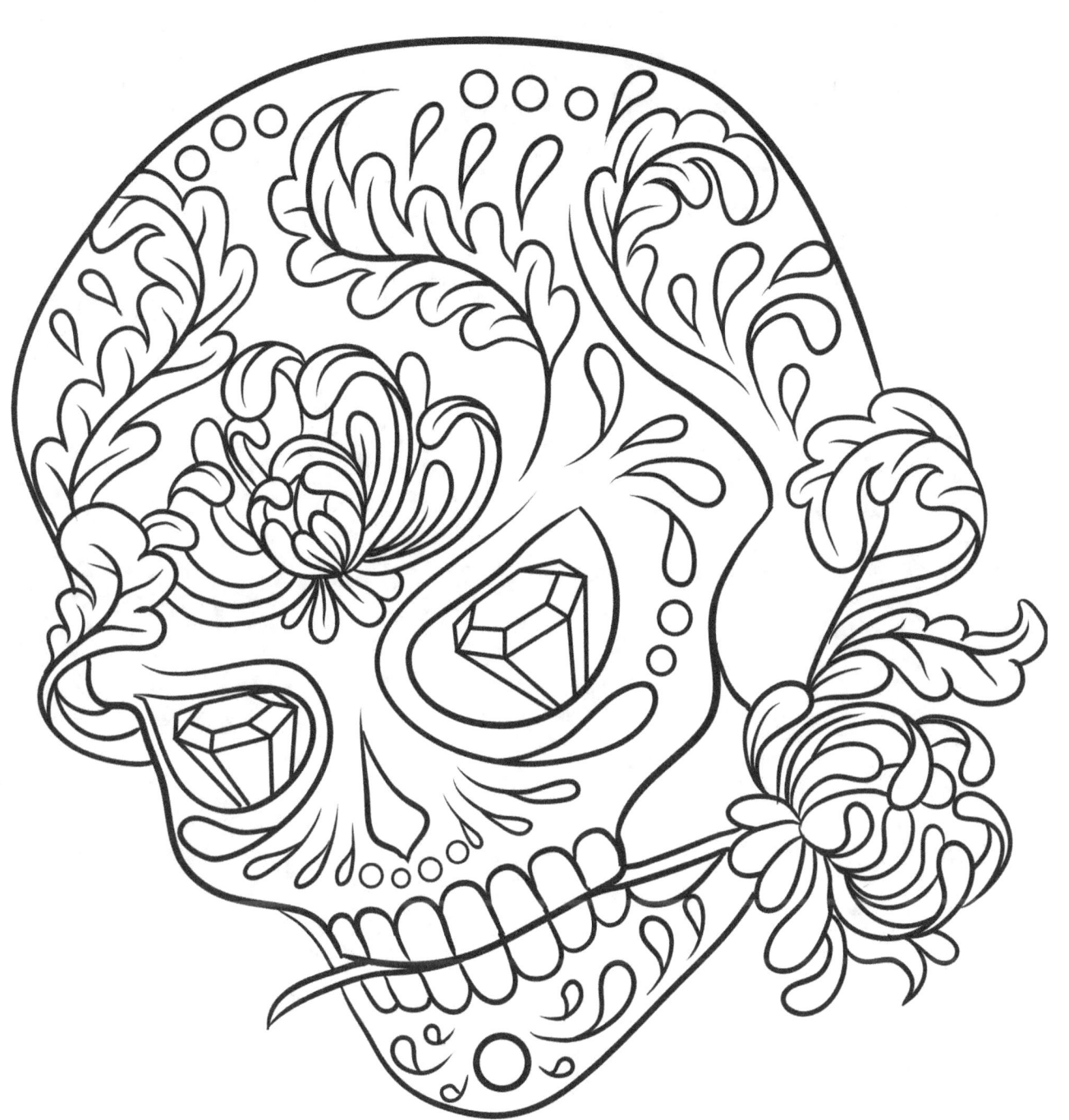

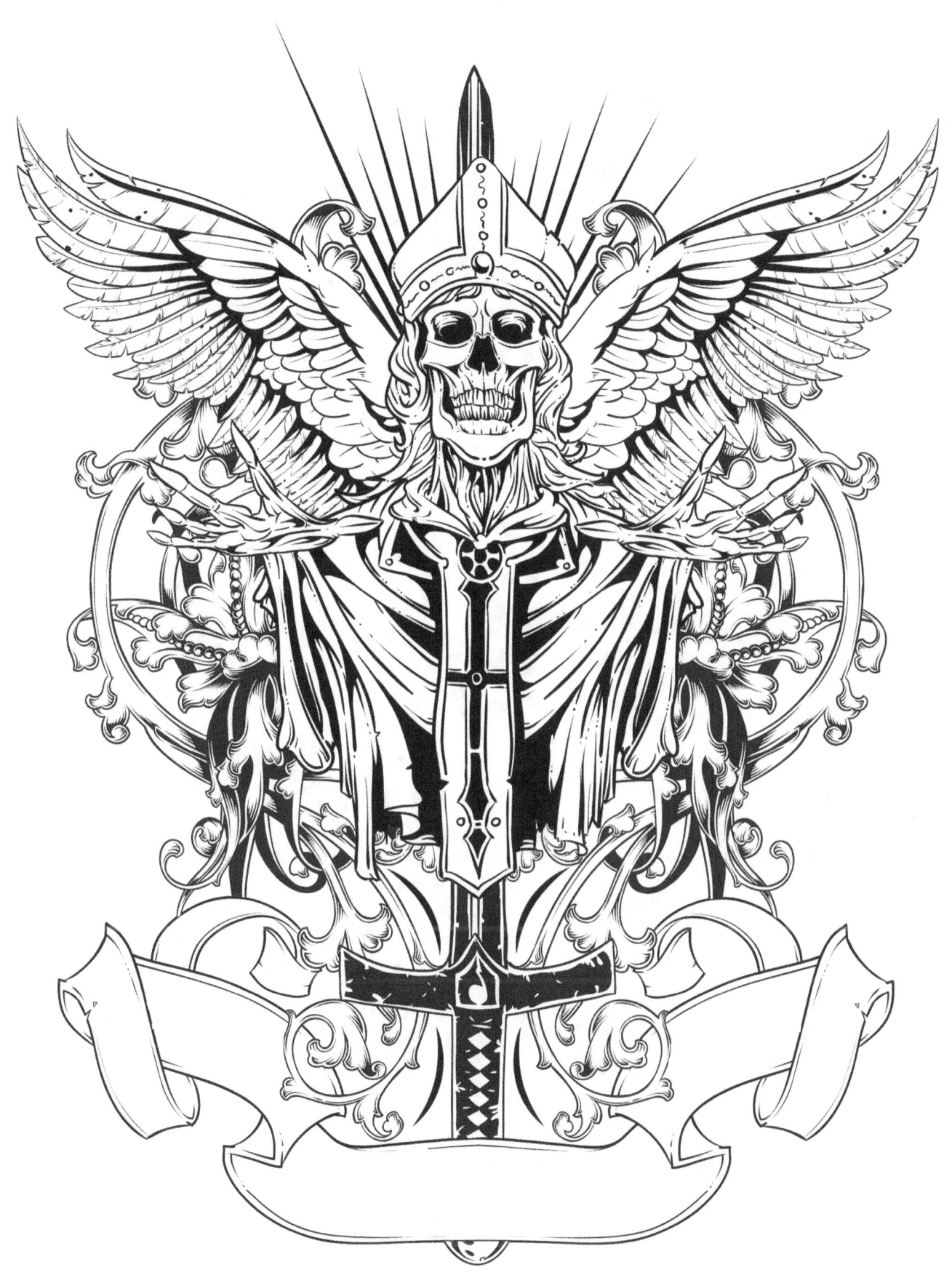

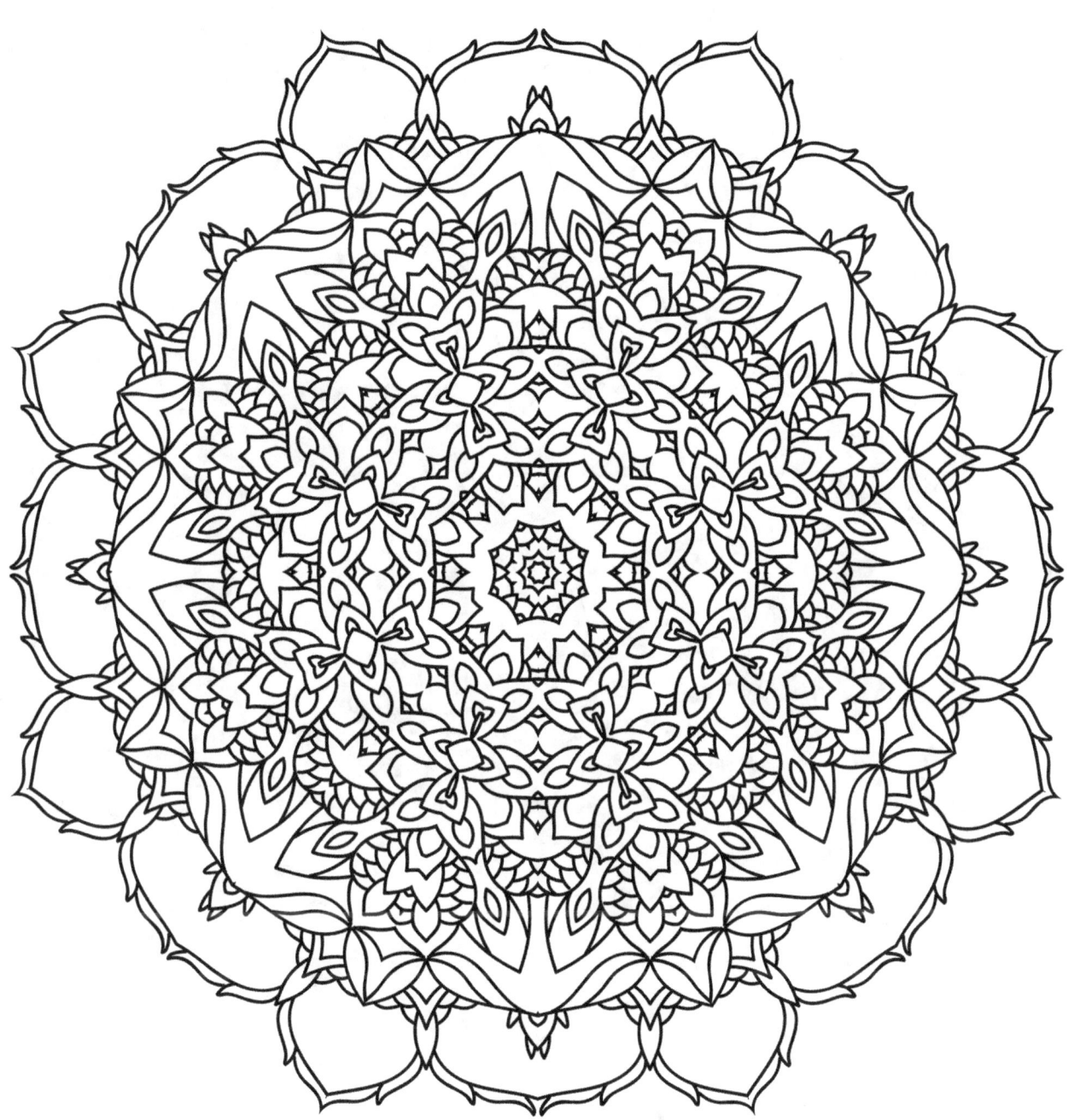

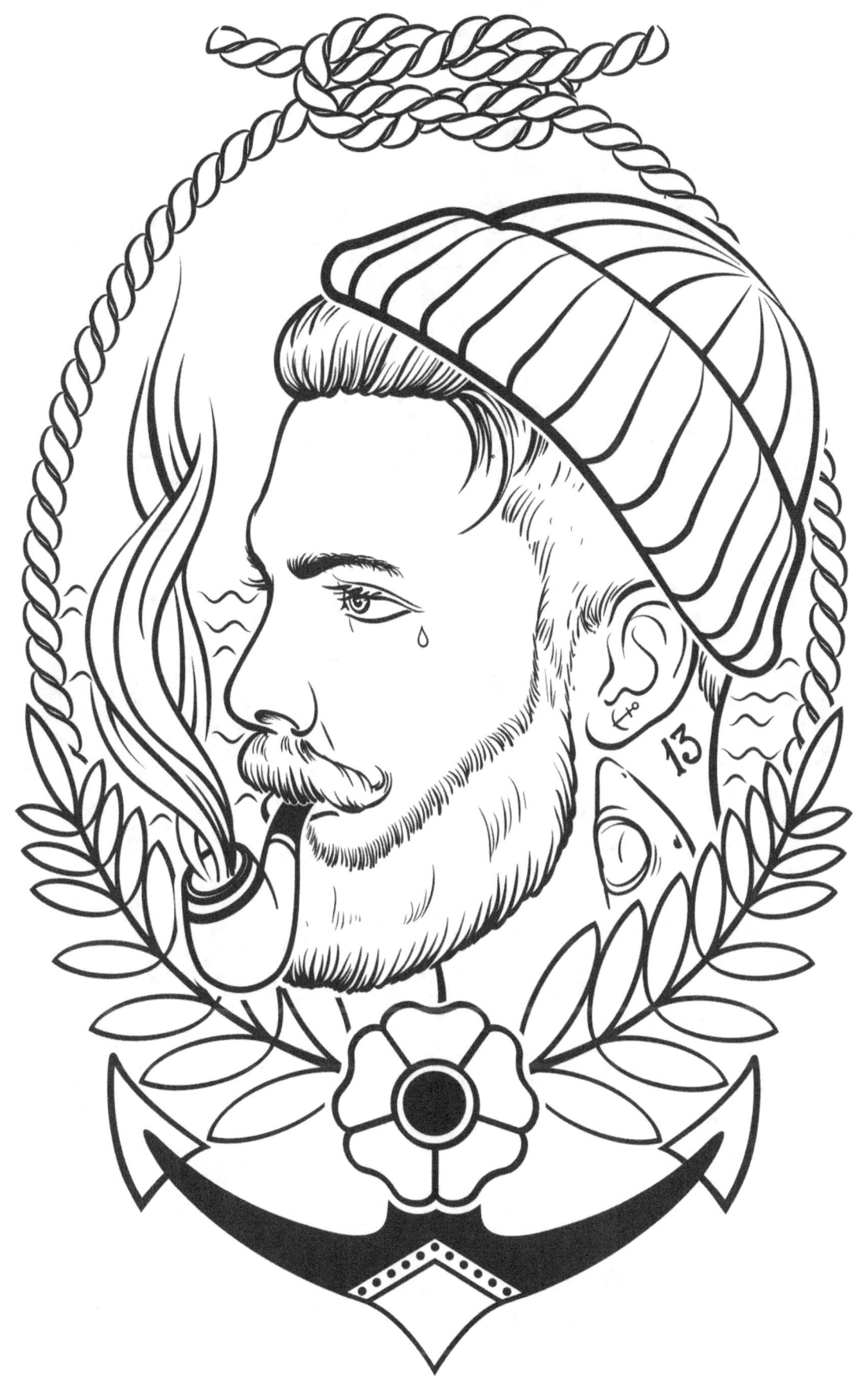

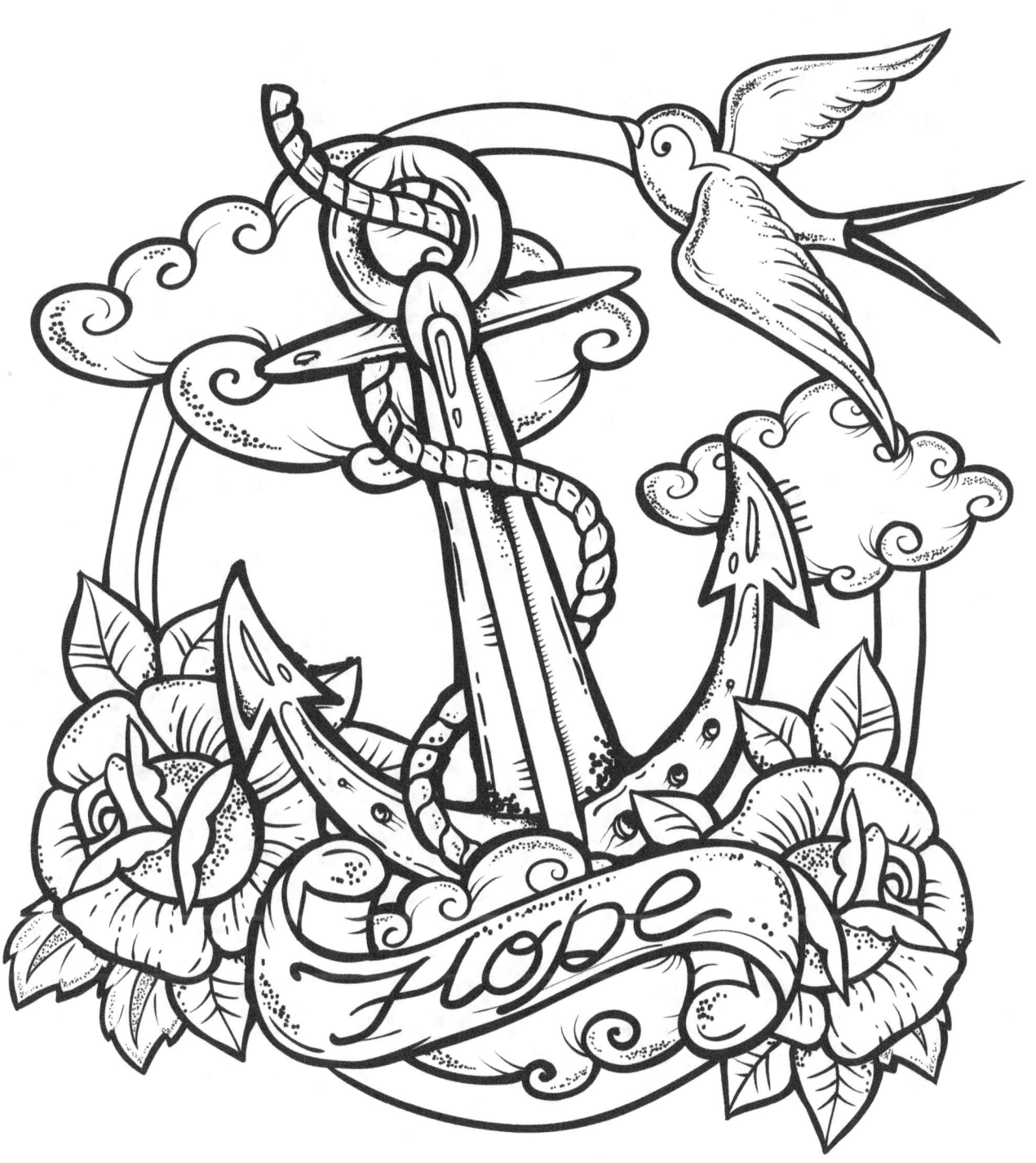

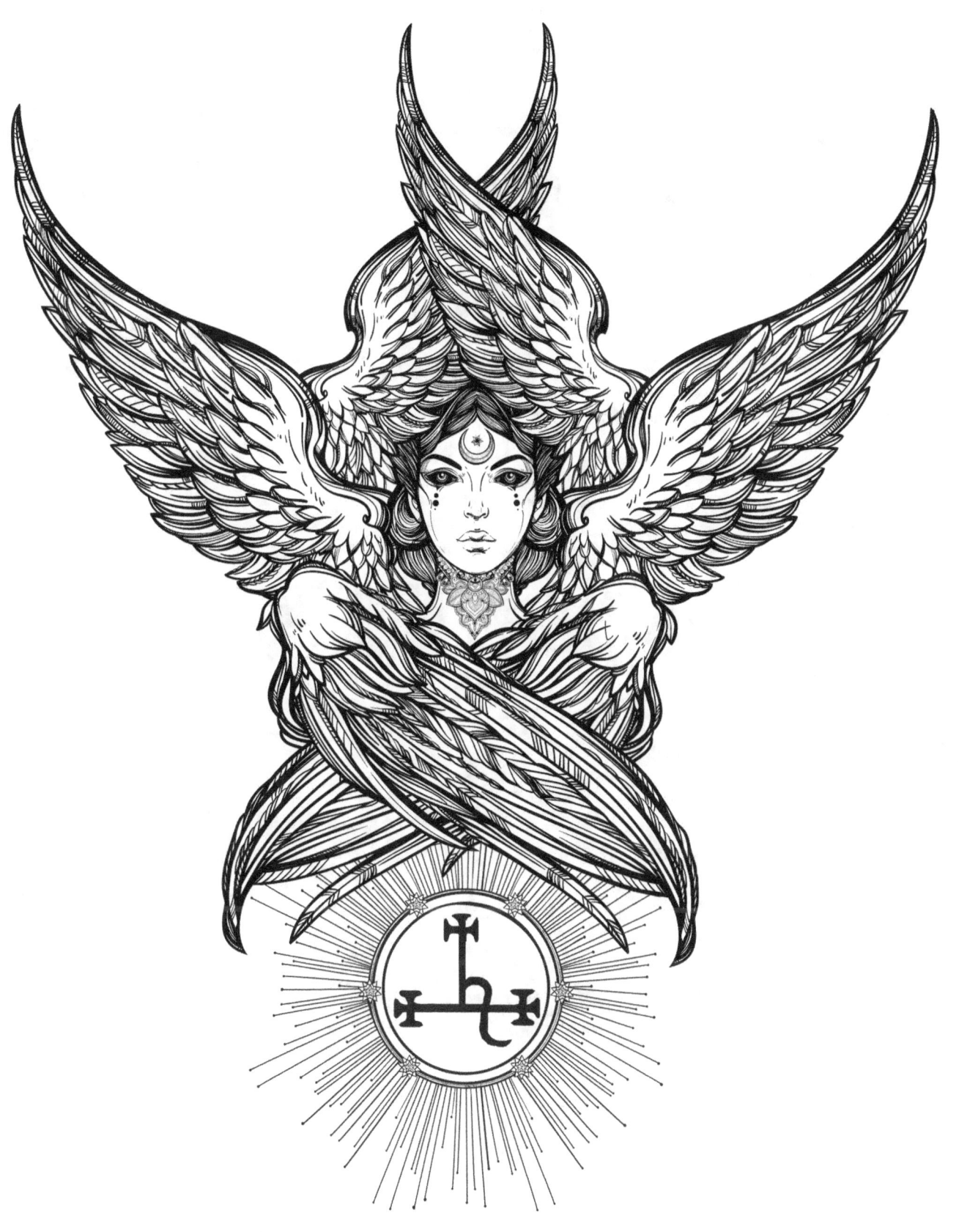

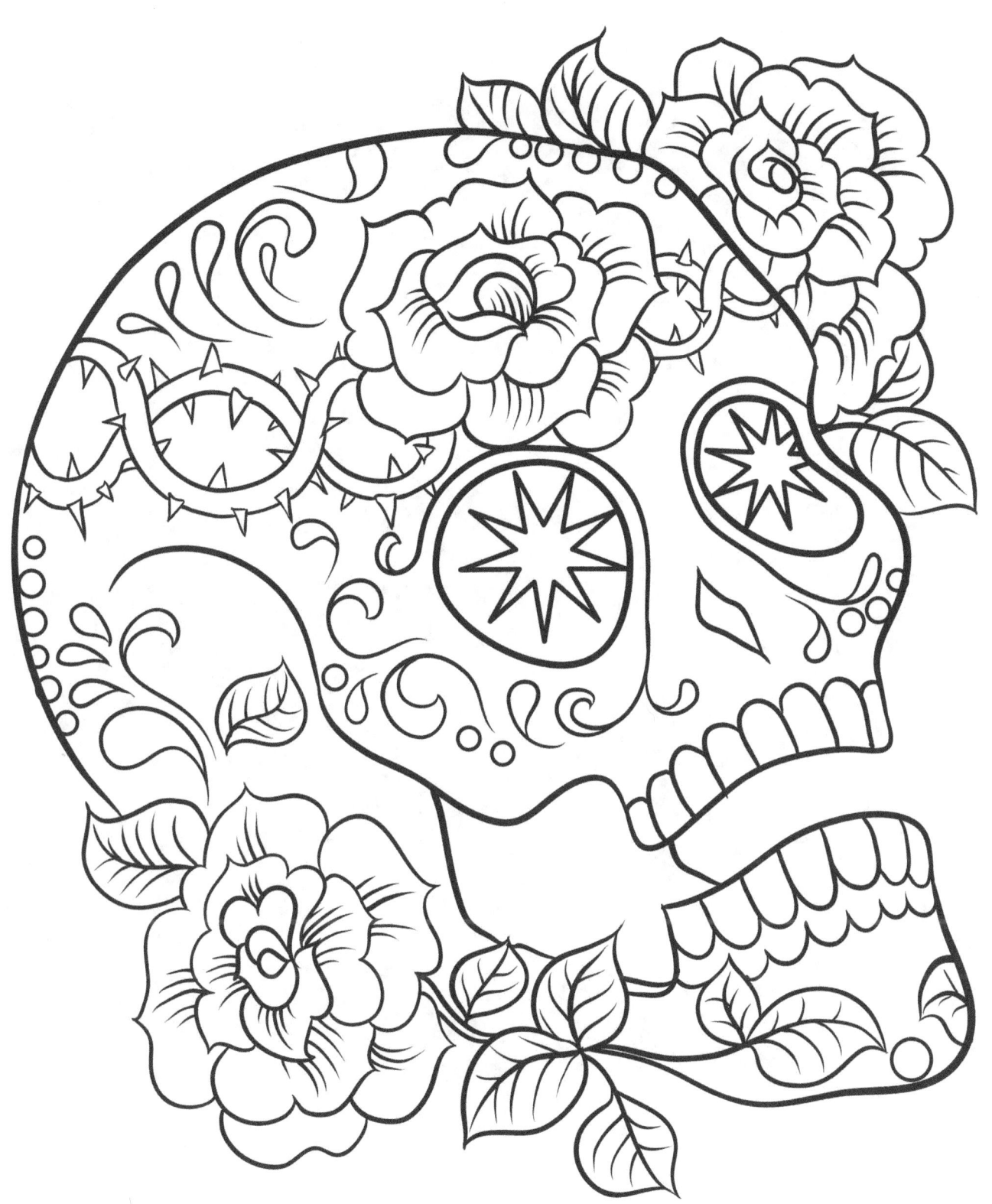

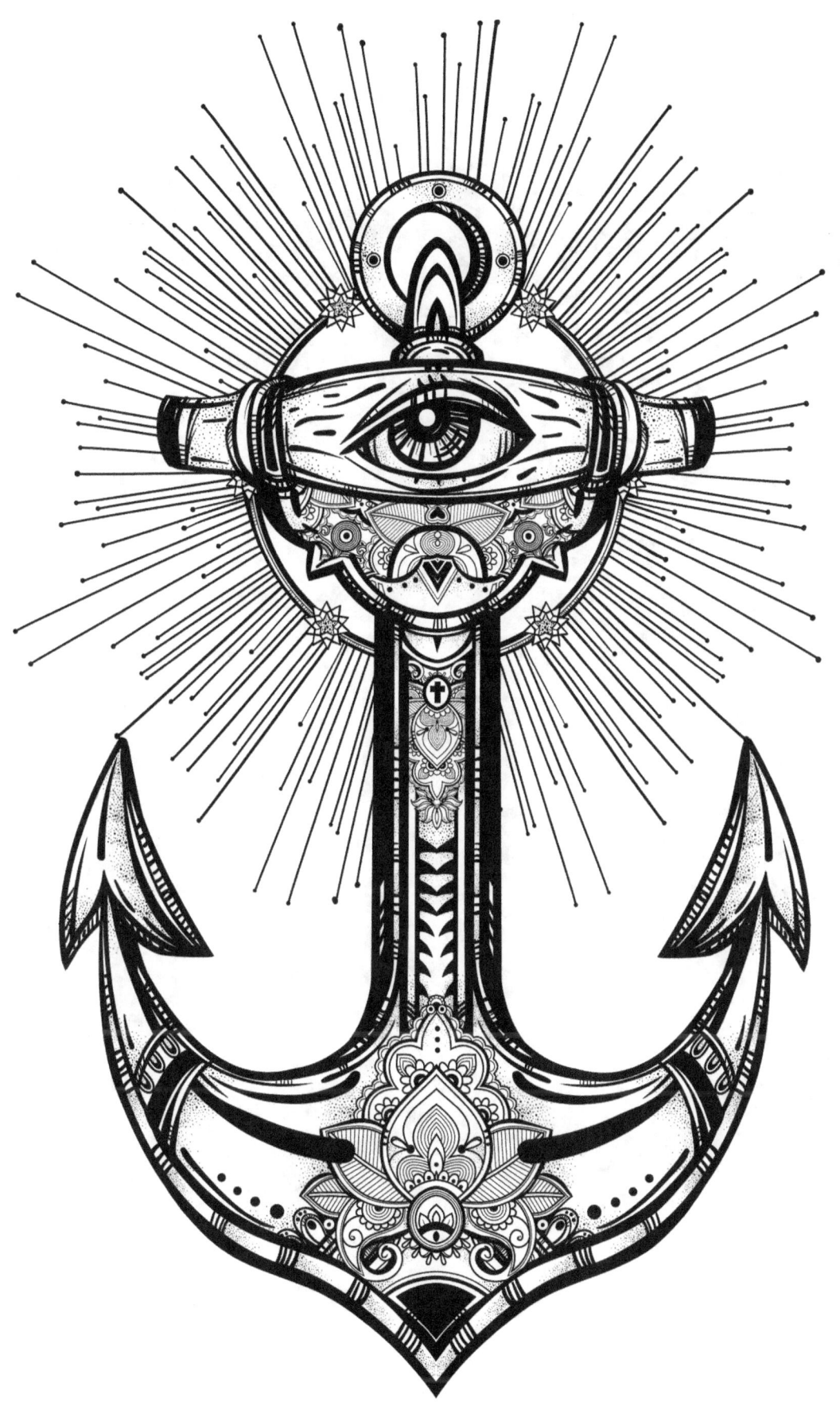

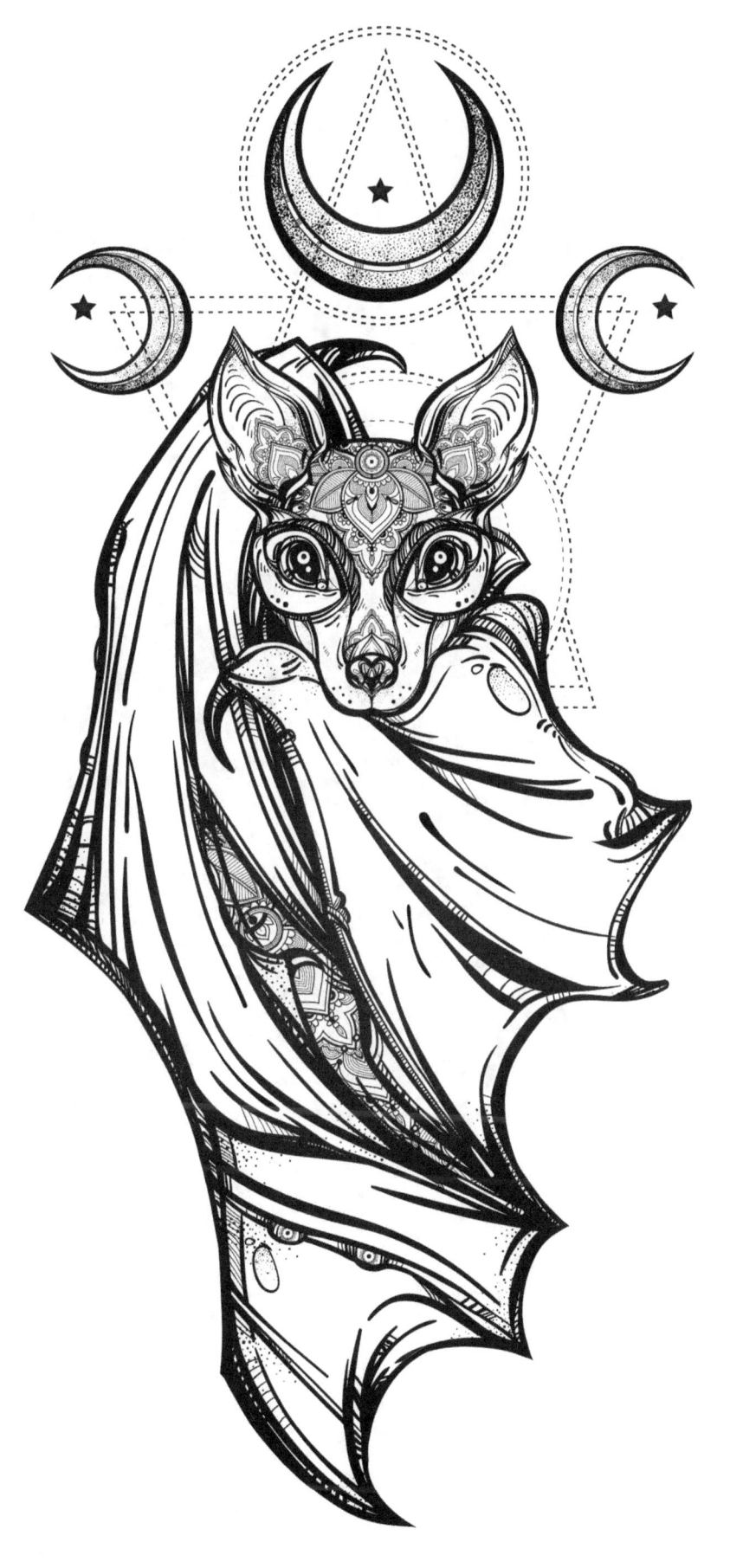

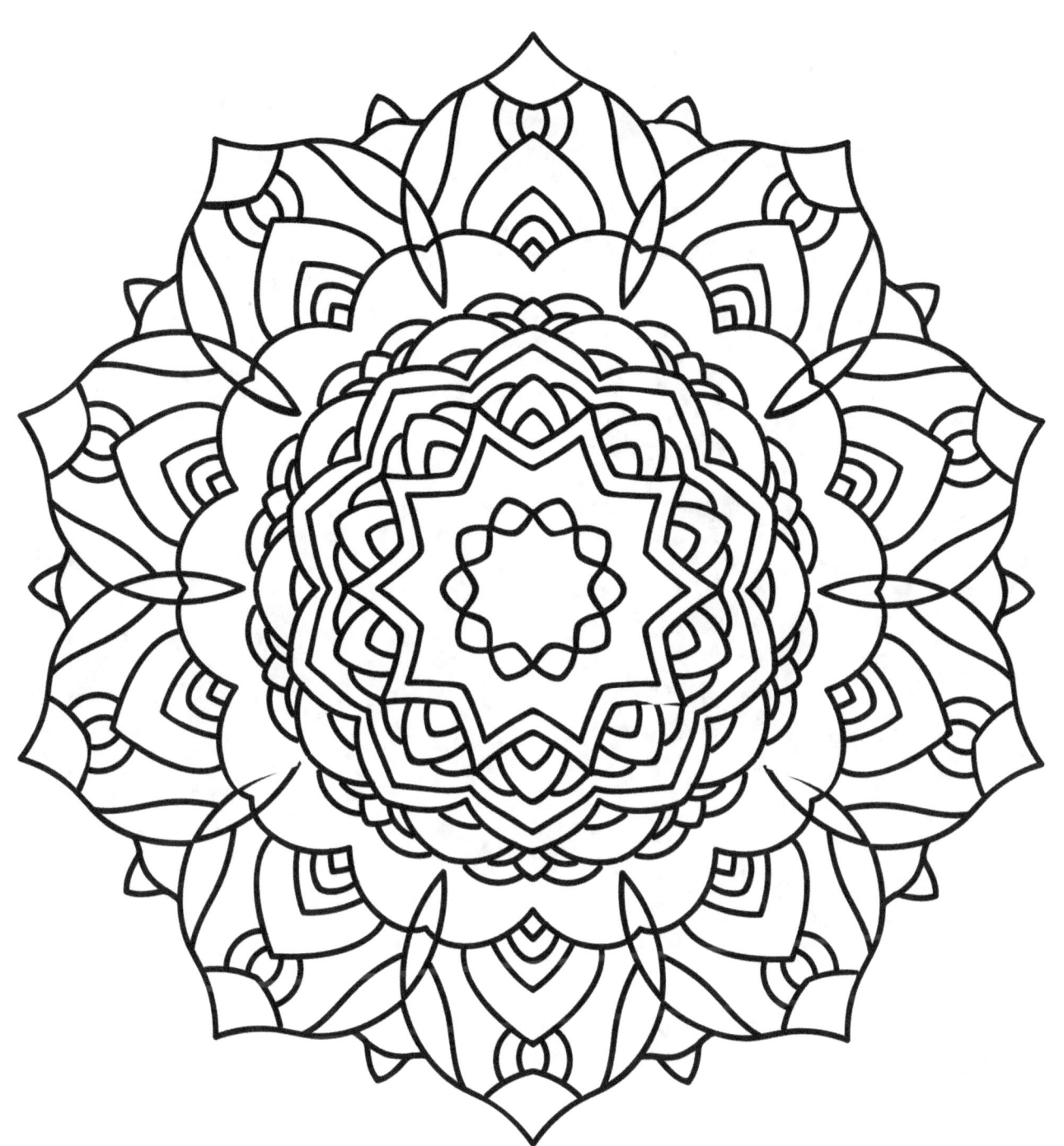

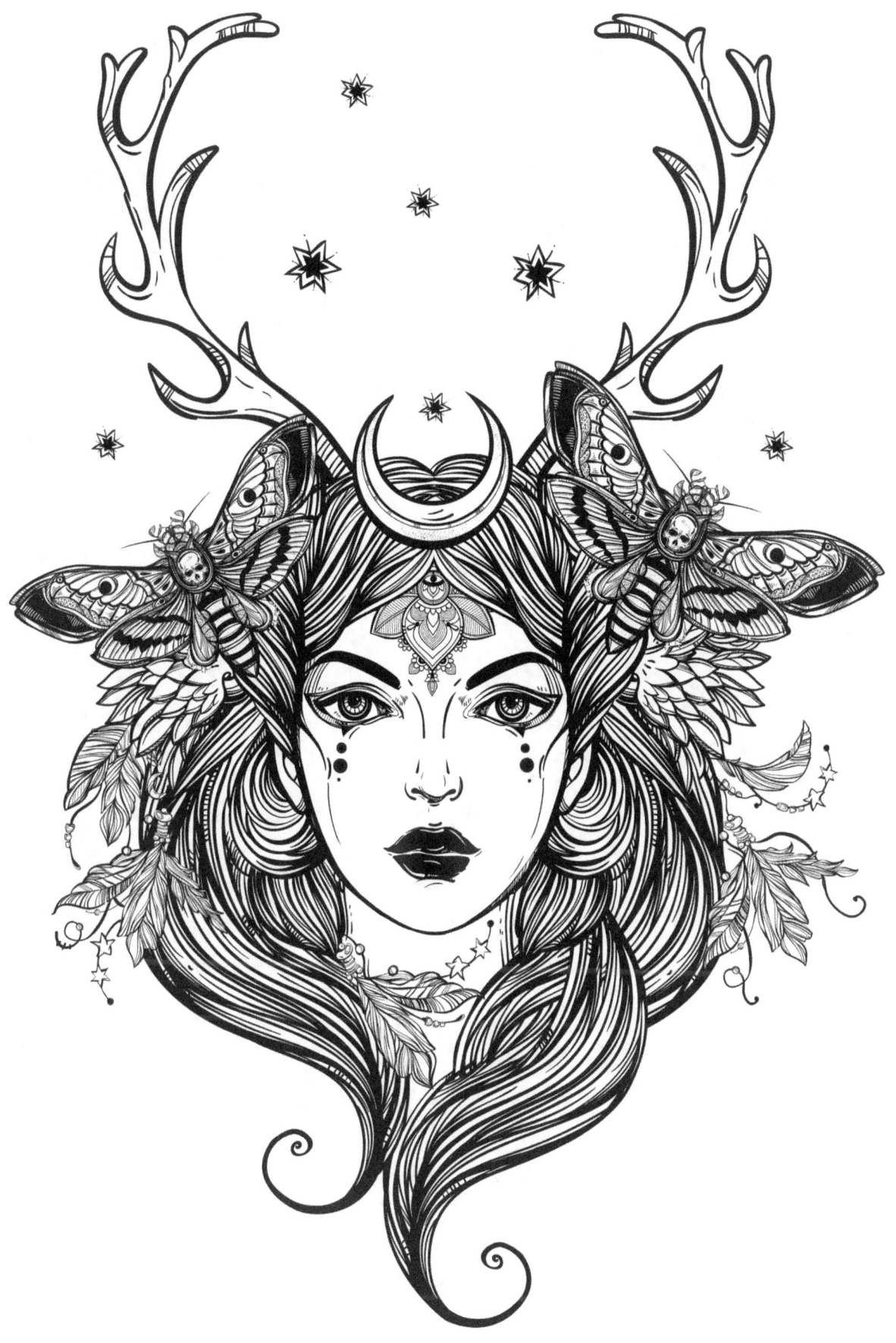

www.ingramcontent.com/pod-product-compliance
Lightning Source LLC
Chambersburg PA
CBHW081558170526
45166CB00009B/2737